Boxgrove: History of a Sussex Village

Written & compiled
to celebrate the Millennium
by The Boxgrove History Group

John Luffingham
Tim Pullan
Nina Small
Robert Thom
Iris Watts

Editor John Luffingham

Proceeds from the sale of this book, after the costs of production and further printing have been met, will be donated to local charities.

Published 2000 by The Boxgrove History Group, Broadlands, Halnaker, Chichester PO18 0NQ
Printed and bound by L&S Printing Company Limited, Worthing, West Sussex.

ISBN 0-9537663-0-6

Acknowledgements

The authors gratefully acknowledge generous financial support from the following organisations without whose help this book could not have been published

Skyforce Avionics Ltd.,
5 The Old Granary, Boxgrove, Chichester

Millennium Festival – Awards for all Grant
from The Heritage Lottery Fund

The Marc Fitch Fund
5 Murray Court, Banbury Road, Oxford

West Sussex County Council, Chichester

Pictorial Acknowledgements

Illustrations are reproduced by kind permission of the following:-

The Ordnance Survey ©Crown Copyright NC99/076, Fig. 1.

English Heritage, Photographic Library. Figs. 2,3,5 & Plate I, Cover image of Boxgrove Man.

Pearson Education Ltd. from 'The Southeast to AD1000' by Peter Drewett, Figs. 4 & 9

Cambridge University Collection of Air Photographs: Copyright reserved, Fig. 7.

Mary Parker, Southdown Promotions, Plate II

Christopher Zeuner, The Weald and Downland Museum, Figs. 10,11,21.

Phaidon Press, Fig. 12

David Bathurst, from 'Around Chichester', Sutton Publishing Ltd., Figs. 15,40,44,45,46.

Malcolm Knight, Sealand Aerial Photography Ltd., Plates III, XXVI.

The British Library, 7815 AAA1, Fig. 16.

Sister Concordia Scott and Sister Mary Marshall, St Mary's Abbey, West Malling, Fig. 17.

Tom Cotton, Plates, V, VI, VII, VIII, IX, X, XI

The National Portrait Gallery, London, Plates, XII, XIII, XIV, XV, XVI. Figs. 27,29,32.

Henry Uniacke, Plate IV.

David Goodman, Figs. 22,23,34,35. Plates XXIV, XXV.

The Trustees of the Goodwood Collection, Plates XVII, XIX, XX, XXI, XXII, cover image of Goodwood House, Figs.33,48,49.

Mrs F.W. Steer, Figs.24,25.

Harry Margary Maps, Lympne Castle, Kent CT21 4LQ, The West Sussex Record Office and the County Archivist Fig. 26 (PM249 3B), Fig. 28, (PM249 5).

Bodleian Library, University of Oxford, Ms.Bodl.264, fol.22r detail of lower border, Fig. 31,

Marylebone Cricket Club, London UK/Bridgeman Art Library, Plate XXIII.

The West Sussex Record Office and the County Archivist, Figs. 36,37.

Pailthorpe, R. and Serraillier, I. from 'Goodwood Country', Sutton Publishing Ltd.,

Figs. 39,41,43,50

Richard Rundle, Fig. 19, Cover image of Priory.

The Transport Publishing Company, Fig. 47.

FOREWORD
by the Duke of Richmond

I am delighted to have been asked to write a foreword to this interesting book. My family first became associated with Boxgrove when the first Duke bought a hunting box at Goodwood in 1697 to hunt with the Charlton Hunt. It was the third Duke who greatly expanded the Estate in the latter half of the eighteenth century and many of the old flint cottages in Boxgrove were built at that time. Some have been sold, but others remain in the family's possession today, housing Estate employees and pensioners. After the Second World War the Estate built some twelve houses in Park Lane and eight bungalows in St. Blaise's Road, and these remain in the Estate Company's ownership, mostly housing Estate pensioners. The association between Boxgrove Priory and the Gordon Lennox family had grown steadily closer over the years. At least since the fifth Duke's time in the middle of the nineteenth century, the family has worshipped regularly in Boxgrove Priory. The East window was erected to his memory by the tenants of the Estate, and there are windows and memorials in the church to both the seventh Duchesses, to the eighth Duke and his elder son, and to the ninth Duke and Duchess. Most of the earlier Dukes were buried in Chichester Cathedral, but the eighth Duchess, my grandmother, is buried in the far south-east corner of the churchyard. For several generations the Dukes have been patrons of Boxgrove Priory and Trustees of the Countess of Derby's Almshouses.

Originally the Estate owned and farmed all the agricultural land in the parish, but now it is restricted to the land on the west side of The Street and on both sides of the A285, south of the crossroads.

My father used to tell a story about his elder brother. The family left for church in Boxgrove one Sunday morning, but because he was still eating his breakfast, my father's brother was late and as a result stole the housemaid's bicycle and set off for Boxgrove on the most direct route. On throwing the bicycle over the flint wall near Molecomb Stud, the front wheel buckled and he walked home carrying the bicycle. When my grandmother returned from Church she confronted her son. 'Darling, you've broken my heart', she said. 'I don't know about your heart, but I've broken the housemaid's bicycle!' he replied.

What of the future of Boxgrove and our family's relationship to it? Over the next twenty-five years I predict that there may be significant housing development in Boxgrove, especially to the east of the parish; the bus service may come steadily under pressure and might disappear; the shop may have real difficulty in remaining viable; the cost of maintaining the fabric of the Priory will substantially increase; the church may be joined with another neighbouring parish with the vicar looking after both; the village hall and club may be renovated and expanded and become more of a community centre; the number of elderly people and the average age in the parish may increase, the number of voluntary organisations, especially for the young, may grow; almost every house may have a computer and access to the Internet; the number of cars travelling through the village may sharply increase; our family may still be living in Goodwood House and owning the Goodwood Estate; there may be fewer Estate staff and pensioners living in Goodwood houses and these houses may be let to other people; some houses may be built by a Housing Association to let at 'affordable' rents; the value of houses may rise sharply; because of the increased housing the school may be expanded further; because of the increase of old people there may be more housing built especially for them.

Not only do time change but the rate of change itself increases. However, this part of Sussex will surely remain a desirable place to live and many people drawn to the area may care to know something of those who were here before them. I warmly commend this book to everyone interested in Boxgrove, either as a resident, or a visitor to the Priory, or to Chichester.

Richmond

CONTENTS

Textual Acknowledgements

Permission to reproduce the excerpts on page 38 from 'Life and Campaigns of the Black Prince' by Richard Barber has been kindly granted by Boydell and Brewer Ltd., Woodbridge, Suffolk.

'Ha'naker Mill' by Hilaire Belloc, from 'Complete Verse of Hilaire Belloc' published by Random House, UK. Ltd., is reproduced by kind permission of the Peters, Fraser and Dunlop Group Ltd.

Included in "Memories of Village Life" are tape recorded interviews with Boxgrove residents conducted and edited by Wendy Austin-Ward. These have been reproduced by kind permission of Wendy Austin-Ward and the Boxgrove Women's Institute.

The authors are grateful to the Sussex Archaeological Society for permission to reproduce the plan of Boxgrove Priory and excerpts from the following:

Volumes of the Sussex Archaeological Collections.

SAC 10 1858	Nicholls, J.G. 'The Progress of Edward VI in Sussex'.
SAC 43 1900	Andre, J.L. 'Halnaker House'
SAC 86 1947	Barker, E.E. 'Anglo Saxon Charters'
SAC 97 1959	Fleming, L. 'Lessay Abbey, Mother House of Boxgrove Priory'.
SAC 110 1972	McCann, T. and Wilkinson, P. 'The Cricket Match at Boxgrove in 1622'.

The following maps are reproduced by courtesy of the Directors of the Goodwood Estate Company Limited and with acknowledgements to the West Sussex Record Office and the County Archivist.

Plate XVII	Map of Halnaker, 1629 (Goodwood MS. E4981)
Figure 33	Yeakell and Gardiner Map, 1781 (Goodwood MS. E30)
Figure 36	25 in. OS Map S..LX11/1, 1875 (Goodwood MS.E5051)
Figure 37	25 in. OS Map S. XL1X/13, 1875 (Goodwood MS.E5051)

The authors wish to thank the following people for advice and assistance.

James Pickford	Boxgrove
Andrew Foster	University College, Chichester
Rosemary Andreae	Curator, Goodwood House
Timothy McCann	West Sussex County Record Office
Rosemary Eveson	National Portrait Gallery
Wendy Austin-Ward	Boxgrove Women's Institute
Vera Quinton	Boxgrove Women's Institute
Phyllis Norrell	Boxgrove
Molly Joyce	Boxgrove
Cathy Houghton	English Heritage
Jennie Fordham	English Heritage
Christopher Zeuner	Weald and Downland Museum
David Goodman	Boxgrove
Elizabeth Pullan	Boxgrove
Elizabeth Luffingham	Halnaker
Joan Jenkyns	Arundel
Marjorie Hollowood	Walberton
Emma Young	Sussex Archaeological Society
Gwen Jones	Editor, Sussex Archaeological Collections
Alistair McAlpine	Tangmere
Sue Wells	Boxgrove
Richard Hunt	Halnaker

PREFACE

This book has been produced in the hope that it will prove of interest to the general reader. Many books already exist covering the history of the whole county and it has therefore been the intention of the present authors to focus on the parish of Boxgrove and Halnaker and to gather together information closely relating to that limited area.

A wide range of sources have been consulted but because of the general nature of the text it has not been thought appropriate to use footnotes or quote references. Instead, the reader wishing to delve further into the subject matter of each chapter is referred to a short bibliography.

Sources that have proved of especial value have been 'The Victoria County History of Sussex, Dallaway's 'History of West Sussex' and many volumes of the Sussex Archaeological Collections. The staff of the West Sussex County Record Office have been unfailingly helpful in providing advice and access to Diocesan Records, Boxgrove School Records, Parish magazines and many other sources.

No claim is made for any originality in the material presented which is of the nature of an anthology of writing relating to Boxgrove and Halnaker that has already been published. The authors have made every attempt to confirm accuracy but must take collective responsibility for any errors.

The size of the subject matter addressed has inevitably meant that there are large time gaps in the story presented. We hope that, in spite of this, readers will find as much interest as we have done in putting this work together.

Bibliography

General

Armstrong, J.R. 'A History of Sussex' 4th Ed. Phillimore 1995

Page, W. and Salzman, L. 'The Victoria History of the Counties of England, Sussex', University of London Press 1973.

Nairn, I, and Pevsner, N. 'The Buildings of England, Sussex', Penguin Press 1965.

Dallaway, J., 'A history of the western division of the county of Sussex including the rapes of Chichester, Arundel and Bramber with the city and diocese of Chichester'. Bensley, London. 1915

Boxgrove Man

Pitts, M and Roberts, M., 'Fairweather Eden, Life in Britain half a million years ago as revealed by the excavations at Boxgrove', Century 1977.

Boxgrove from the Mesolithic to the Iron Age

Drewett, P.L., Rudling, D. and Gardiner,M., 'The South East to AD 1000', Longman, 1988.

Boxgrove in Roman & Saxon Times

Dark, K and P., 'The Landscape of Roman Britain', Sutton Publishing, 1997.

Place Names in the Parish of Boxgrove

Mawer, A and Stenton, F.M., 'The place names of Sussex', Cambridge University Press,1929.

The Coming of the Normans

Bede (Trs.Sherley-Price) 'A History of the English Church and People', Penguin 1955.

Brandon, P. and Short, B. 'The South East from AD 1000' Longman 1990.

Morris, J., 'Domesday Book-Sussex', Phillimore 1976.

A Holy Relic at Halnaker

Andre, J.L., 'Halnaker House' Sussex Archaeological Collections 43, 1900.

Gunner,W.H., 'The Will of Lucas de Ponynges', Archaeological Journal II,1845.

A Benedictine Community

Knowles, D., 'Bare Ruined Choirs', Cambridge University Press,1976.

The British Library, 'The Benedictines in Britain', British Library,1980.

The Dissolution of the Priory

Dickens, A.G., 'The English Reformation', Collins,1964.

Duffy, G., 'The Stripping of the Altars',York University Press, New Haven 1922.

The King visits Halnaker

Nicholls, J.G., 'The progress of Edward VI in Sussex', Sussex Archaeological Collections 10, 1858.

Halnaker Mill

Brunnarius, M., 'The Windmills of Sussex', Phillimore,1979.

The Morleys of Halnaker

Steer, F. W., 'A short history and description of Halnaker house'. Privately printed 1958. Available in Chichester Reference Library.

Johnson, O., 'The Sussex Tree Book',Pomegranate Press 1998.

Cricket at Boxgrove

McCann, T and Wilkinson, P. 'The Cricket Match at Boxgrove in 1622'. Sussex Archaeological Collections, 110.1972.

Marshal, J., 'Sussex Cricket, a history', Heinemann 1959.

The Ascendancy of Goodwood

Reese, M. M., 'Goodwood's Oak, The Life and Times of the Third Duke of Richmond, Lennox and Aubigny'. Threshold Books. 1987.

Kent, J., 'Records and reminiscences of Goodwood and the Dukes of Richmond'. Samson Low,1896.

The Charlton Hunt

Rees, S., 'The Charlton Hunt', Phillimore,1988.

The Council Speaks

Porter, V., 'Village Parliaments', Phillimore 1994.

INTRODUCTION

The village of Boxgrove in West Sussex lies on the coastal plain just below the South Downs and three miles east of the city of Chichester. Its village street has some interesting stone cottages which blend well with the red brick houses of a more recent date. It has at its centre, the village store and Post Office, the Priory Church, a primary school founded in 1741, and some interesting almshouses founded at the same time by the same benefactor. About seven

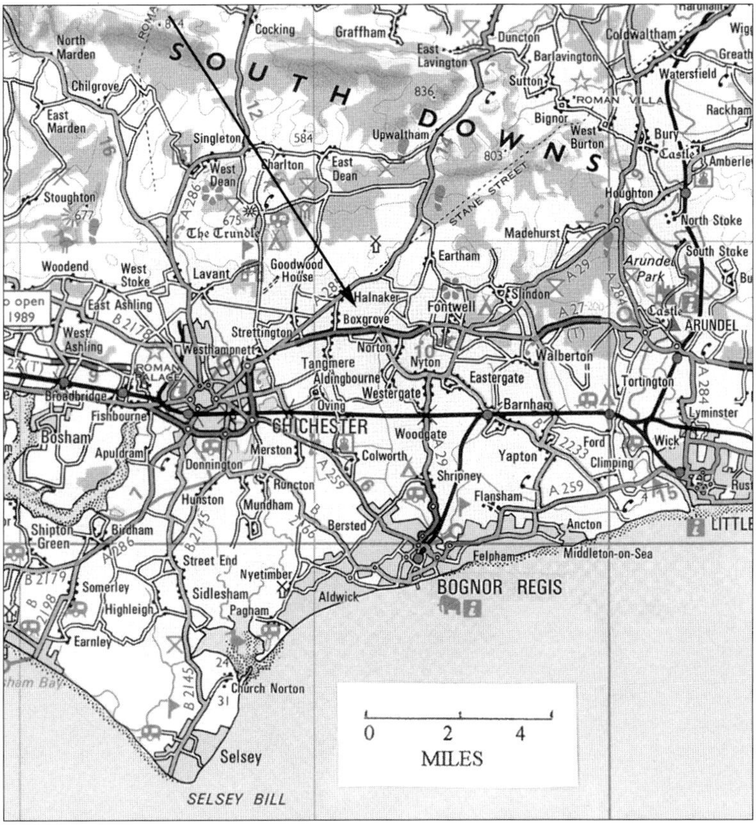

Figure 1 The location of Boxgrove

hundred and thirty people live in the village which is surrounded by farmland. Half a mile north lies the hamlet of Halnaker, once a separate community but now with only an inn and a blacksmith's shop remaining amongst the houses, it is included within the parish of Boxgrove. Halnaker House, once the seat of

Lord De La Warr lord of the manor in the sixteenth century, now lies in ruins. Patronage of the village has long been in the hands of the Dukes of Richmond from their seat at Goodwood House, one mile to the north west. Opportunities for local employment arise on the Goodwood estate in relation to farming, game and forest management, the Goodwood race course and in connection with the many activities surrounding a stately home open to the public. The Annual Festival of Speed instituted by the Earl of March and his revival of the classic motor racing meetings on the circuit surrounding Goodwood airfield bring thousands of visitors to the area with consequent demands for accommodation. There is a large hotel and Country Club at Goodwood Park and many local residents provide bed and breakfast accommodation. Surrounding farms crop wheat and oil seed rape as well as grazing sheep and there is an intensive horticultural operation growing lettuces for the supermarkets. There are several stud farms and in Halnaker a large poultry processing plant provides employment for about two hundred and thirty staff. Recently Boxgrove has been chosen as head office for a successful aircraft avionics company. Many villagers of course work in Chichester and further afield and many other residents are living here in retirement.

Boxgrove is mentioned in the Domesday Book. How did it arise and how has the life of the villagers changed over the ages? There are many historical incidents relating to the area which give a series of snapshots of village life at particular moments in history. There are, however, long blank periods when nothing specific is known of Boxgrove itself. In this history we have tried to fill in some of these blanks by informed guesswork using information relating to similar communities. By this means we hope to illustrate how life in the village would have altered from its early settlement up to the present day. The story starts five hundred thousand years ago with Boxgrove Man whose remains were recently discovered within half a mile of the village.

BOXGROVE MAN

On 17 May 1994 Boxgrove in West Sussex made headline news when it was reported that part of an early human tibia (shin bone), some half a million years old, had been discovered during an archaeological excavation in a gravel pit there. As *The Times* put it 'English Heritage finds the oldest human in Europe - and he is English!' This exciting discovery came in the year English Heritage celebrated its tenth anniversary, just as funding for the archaeological work at Boxgrove was due to end.

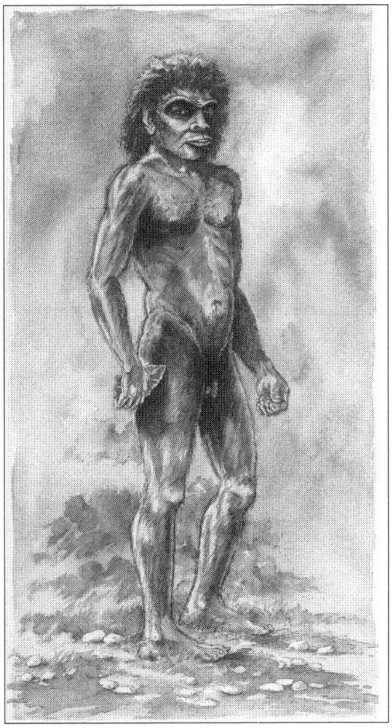

Figure 2. An artist's impression of what the Boxgrove hominid may have looked like.

The tibia was found as this unique site was closing in November 1993. By late December it had been confirmed as coming from a hominid, an early human individual, and in May 1994 the news was made public. Boxgrove Man's tibia is not complete, both ends are missing but the remaining piece is approximately thirty centimetres in length, and from its dimensions experts consider it to be from a male hominid about six feet in height and weighing about 80-90 kilograms (12-13 stone). Modern technology may eventually make it possible to estimate the age at death of the hominid from which it came half a million years ago.

Figure 3. A view of the Boxgrove quarry, where the archæological finds were made.

After this discovery English Heritage decided to fund a further two years' investigative excavation at the quarry, in the hope that more of 'Boxgrove Man' would come to light. It did, when another important find was made. In September 1995, in a freshwater deposit, two hominid teeth were discovered. They were two lower incisors from the same individual. There were diagonal scratch marks across the front of both teeth, running from the top left to the bottom right, probably these marks came from a flint tool being drawn repeatedly across the teeth as the hominid sliced meat, or perhaps hide, that he held clamped in his jaws. The teeth are very worn, and tartar has built up, possibly preserving particles of food. Analysis of the tartar may provide evidence of the diet available to these early inhabitants of the West Sussex coastal plain. The incisors were found in a lower geological layer than the shin bone and are thought to be older by only a few hundred years or even less.

The earliest members of the hominid family belong to a period of time known as the Palaeolithic (Old Stone Age) because the majority of worked objects we have from that time are made from stone; these artefacts range in age from two and a half million down to ten thousand years old. Anthropologists have identified the tibia as belonging to the species *Homo* cf *heidelbergensis*, a species characterized by its robusticity and extremely large jaws. It is believed to be ancestor to the Neanderthals, who evolved 300,000 years ago, but not to our species, *Homo sapiens*, who first appeared in Africa around 130,000 years ago,

Between groups in early man there occurred many differences in build: a fascinating and unexpected pattern of physical diversity is revealed amongst the various groups making up very early populations. There were differences in their robustness (thick features) and gracility (fine features or slender physique), their skulls, brow ridges and limb bones. Differences in size and development of their brains were also discovered: *Homo erectus*, who first appeared in Africa about two million years ago, was of robust build and his brain was two-thirds the size of modern brains. *Homo erectus* was able to make and use stone tools.

The Boxgrove shin bone, on which can be discerned ridges that once held strong muscles, comes from a robustly built hominid adapted to physical strains and an active lifestyle. This hominid fashioned tools: hand-axes were knapped from flint nodules; some have been found in excellent condition, even retaining the fine marks on their cutting edges that indicate the manner in which the axe was used. He butchered animal carcasses in much the same way as butchers do today. Comparisons between the half-million year old and present day animal bones that have been butchered using a hand-axe show marks that are uncannily similar.

There is evidence that the Boxgrove hominid and his companions hunted rather than scavenged for already dead animals, as was previously believed of hominids from this period. This evidence comes from a scapula (shoulder blade) from a horse which was discovered, with a wound that was possibly inflicted by a projectile such as a spear. If the wound does prove to have been made by a spear, it would provide evidence that the Boxgrove group hunted for their meat.

Hunting, especially of larger animals, calls for some kind of organisation and therefore some inter-communication between hunters if the outcome is to be successful.

The *Daily Telegraph* of 29 April, 1998, reported that anthropologists have anatomical evidence that suggests human-like vocal abilities may have appeared in hominids much earlier than has been supposed. Neanderthals are now believed to have been capable of speech. Two hundred thousand years earlier still, the Boxgrove hominid group, organising their hunting, making their hand-axes, butchering and dividing the meat from the kill and seeing off the scavengers such as hyena and wolf, may possibly have needed more than body language and animal-like sounds if they were to co-ordinate their activities successfully. Unless several skulls of these prehistoric people are found, and to date none has been, there is no possible way we can know what speech capabilities if any they possessed.

One of the archaeological puzzles of the palaeolithic period is where these hominids lived. Boxgrove has not provided an answer. No trace of huts or hearths or even holes that might have supported a hide tent has been found. We believe that fire was in use in China during this period, from the evidence of charred embers found near the skull of Peking Man. There is no evidence however that Boxgrove Man was able to use fire. It is probable that the Boxgrove group was nomadic and moved as and when the animals on which they depended for their sustenance migrated. This may have seen them returning to some areas on a seasonal basis, but always trailing the animals, so that a permanent camp would have been of little use. However, large and dangerous carnivores roamed the plain, so that the old and very young, left behind at a base camp, would have needed a guard when the foraging party was away hunting.

There is evidence that hominids remained in the Boxgrove area as weather conditions worsened, but no evidence that they made any sort of clothing. If they did make and use clothing, bone needles, often cited as evidence for this, have not survived. Did they have 'possessions'? One of the most exciting finds at Boxgrove was a hammer made from the base of an antler, which came from a species of giant deer, *Megaloceros dawkinsi*, that became extinct 500,000 years ago. Not only is it the oldest antler hammer in the world, but it also helps to confirm the date the hominids lived in or visited Boxgrove as belonging to the interglacial period that immediately preceded the Anglian ice age about 480,000 years ago. The hammer shows marks of much use: it is extremely well worn and is thought to have helped in the fashioning of a good number of hand-axes. We will never know whether it was the prized possession of one individual or a tool shared between a group of flint knappers. Importantly, this tool was used, kept and re-used time and time again. It has slivers of flint embedded in it, confirming it as a tool used in the process of knapping flint to create a hand-axe and was of more worth, it seems, than many of the hand-axes that had been discarded whilst still in pristine condition.

The flint hand-axes found at Boxgrove were finely and symmetrically made and a number of tools were needed to make them. Stone pebbles were used to strike the flint nodules and remove large flakes, and a softer instrument to remove the thinner flakes, such as a hammer made from bone, wood or antler. Battered pebbles and animal limb bones have been found amongst the flint waste at Boxgrove. In several areas the scatter of flint knappings, or waste material, indicates where a hominid sat to manufacture his hand-axe. In places this waste lies exactly as it first fell, allowing the archaeologists to re-assemble the discarded flakes to re-form the original nodule, the core of which, 500,000 years ago, became a hand-axe. The re-assembly of the flakes also allowed the archaeologists to work out the sequence in which the waste had been struck from the nodule.

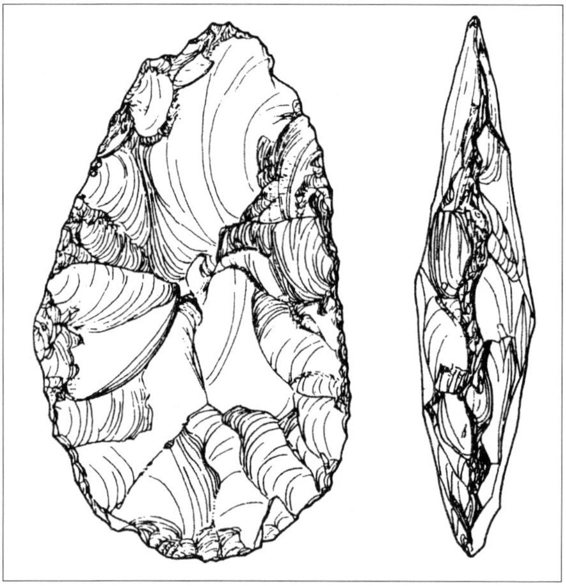

Figure 4. A flint hand-axe found at Boxgrove.

Archaeologists were able to accomplish this reconstruction because the buried land surface upon which the waste had fallen had suffered little, if any, disturbance over the ages. At the horse butchery site, piles of waste flakes appear to indicate that hand-axes were made on the spot for immediate use and taken away afterwards, but in other areas hand axes were being discarded even though still in mint condition. 150 such axes lie abandoned among the butchered remains of rhinoceros, horse, bison and deer, but there is no evidence of flint waste to indicate that the hand axes were manufactured there, so they must have been brought into the area.

All the material found at the Boxgrove excavation is being examined by experts using the most up-to-date technology. Already their laboratory findings reveal flint embedded in the bone of a rhinoceros from the site, and that the marks left by flint tools on some bones were underneath the marks made by the teeth of scavenging animals. Projectile tests on a horse scapula match the damage to the horse scapula discovered at the site and strongly suggest the use of spears in hunting. We begin to get a view of a world inhabited by a group of people whose behaviour was more complex than hitherto imagined. A unique geological sequence made and then preserved this once living landscape.

Figure 5. An artist's impression of the various animals that may have inhabited the Boxgrove site.

Boxgrove is now ten kilometres inland and forty-three metres above sea level, but half a million years ago a high cliff, above a beach of coarse sand and pebbles formed part of a coastline that once extended from what is now Aldingbourne in West Sussex towards Portsmouth and the Isle of Wight area of Hampshire. It was during the climatic fluctuation of the Pleistocene geological epoch, which lasted from around two million until about twelve thousand years ago, that these beaches were formed. They were safeguarded from later coastal erosion by tectonic (earth movement) uplift, which continually occurred during the Pleistocene epoch, raising the land surface relative to the sea level. As the climate became cooler the sea level dropped further, leaving the old Boxgrove beach covered by a deep layer of fine sand (called the Slindon Sands after the nearby village where they were first found).

Eventually the area became an inter-tidal lagoon, which later gradually silted up. The cliff face slowly eroded forming a rubbly slope. In time a soil formed on the surface of the Slindon silts and rubble, developing slowly into a large grassy plain capable of supporting a rich variety of animals, for whom pools of water fed by downland springs provided attractive watering holes. Many of the animal species for whom the Boxgrove plain was home can still be found in Europe today. Some species have become extinct, others are now found only in Africa. Horse, bison, deer and rhinoceros were preyed upon by carnivores which included lions, bears and hyena, and by hominids. Small animals too were present, such as rodents, rabbits and badgers. There were also birds, including duck and geese. During this period the hominid group ranging over this early land surface enjoyed a temperate climate, probably cooler than that of the present, one in which it was not uncomfortable to pursue a physically demanding life style. (See I in colour section)

Towards the end of the Cromerian inter-glacial period the climate started to deteriorate. Vegetation ceased to flourish in the increasingly cold and inclement weather . The grassy plain slowly developed into marshland, rain increased the runoff from the hills, causing still further erosion of the old cliff and carrying silt and rubble over the plain. Peri-glacial conditions (the action of alternate freezing and thawing of the land surface) increased the erosion of the hills beyond the fragile remains of the now-ancient cliff, until mud, flint and gravel slid across the whole area, burying and preserving the prehistoric Boxgrove land surface. This climate change heralded the onset of the coldest period known in this island, the Anglian glaciation, that occurred around 480,000 years ago. How long hominids remained in the area in the face of ever-deteriorating conditions cannot be known, but as carnivorous animals followed herbivores migrating southwards in search of grazing (at this time Britain and the continent were joined by a land bridge) it seems likely that the hominids were drawn away southwards in the wake of the animals they had always relied upon for their food.

The animals of the time are an important factor in determining Boxgrove's relative position within the framework of changing climates, because they evolved as the climate changed. Some species, particularly bears, rhino and small mammals, have become chronological markers, signposts as to where in the ice age timetable different sites should be placed. This is an extremely complex scheme depending on very many comparisons between the animals from many sites across northern Europe: extensive cross-checking is done and many comparisons made, so that the conclusions reached come from very many lines of carefully evaluated evidence, not from a single observation made at one site.

They are a secure method of dating a site. An example from Boxgrove of this comparative approach to dating is provided by water voles. These small mammals lived on the site, they were not hunted nor were they eaten by humans. The teeth of the early water voles had roots until about 600,000 years ago, but it is known from sites elsewhere in England and Europe, for reasons not yet identified, that, as water voles evolved, their teeth became unrooted and continuously-growing. At the Boxgrove site the occurrence of the later forms of water vole, together with the extinct species, leads archaeologists to believe that the finds date from around 500,000 years ago. The minimum age for the site is provided by species such as shrews (*Sorex savini* and *S. runtonensis*), rhino (*Stephanorhinus hundsheimensis*) and the giant deer (*Megaloceros dawkinsi*) that became extinct during the Anglian glaciation around 480,000 years ago. The meticulous retrieval of animal remains at Boxgrove provided the evidence for the complex scheme of dating of the site.

The excavations have ended. The quarry is exhausted commercially and scheduled to be filled and returned to agricultural use, but there is still much to learn from analysis of all the material taken from the site.

It seems then, that the first people to live around Boxgrove were a robust muscular people who formed nomadic groups and lived by hunting the deer, horses and other animals that roamed the coastal plain. There is no evidence that they made clothing or shelters, and they ate their meat raw, but they made excellent flint knives for hunting and butchery. When the glaciers eventually approached and the climate grew too cold they followed the migrating game animals southward into continental Europe, where their progeny may have evolved 200,000 years later into the Neanderthal hominids whose remains have been discovered in the Rhineland.

BOXGROVE FROM THE MESOLITHIC TO THE IRON AGE

Sometime between 7,000 and 8,000 years ago, the earth grew warmer. As the glaciers receded and the climate improved, game moved northwards again and was followed by nomadic hunters. As the icecaps retreated towards the poles, meltwater raised the level of the oceans. To the east large areas of land were flooded extending the North Sea, and southwards where Britain had been connected to the continental landmass, water flooded in joining the Atlantic and the North Sea to form the English Channel: Britain was now an island. Before this time, life would have been little changed since 'Boxgrove Man' and his companions hunted and gathered along the foot of the Downs but excavations at Star Carr in Yorkshire show that by 7000 B.C., more sophisticated hunting methods had been developed including the use of bows and arrows, barbed spears made from antlers and the domestication of dogs for hunting. Flint axes had also been produced allowing the felling of trees and easier shaping of the wood to make shelters.

Bands of nomads ranged along the shores of the Channel. They gradually developed better flint tools, and probably better shelters. There are notable sites at Westhampnett, where flint hand axes and arrowheads were found and at Slindon and Strettington. There is now considerable evidence that about 90% of the country, including the chalk Downs, was covered in mixed deciduous woodland. Oak dominated, among lime, alder, elm and hazel. Native animals included European bison, wild ox, beaver, brown bear, wolf, and wild boar as well as many of our present day small mammals such as fox, badger, and mole. There were no rabbits although they had been present in Boxgrove Man's time.

We should not fall into the trap of thinking that these peoples were totally primitive, just because they used flint tools and simple shelters. They probably lived in tribal groups of extended families with a base camp and other gathering camps perhaps 10 kilometres apart in a roughly permanent territory of about 100 square kilometres. By about 4,000 B.C. Man was beginning to make an impact on the environment by clearing the edges of the forest. Communities began to give up the nomadic life and settle. Finds of carbonised seeds and the pollen grains of wheat and barley indicate early farming and there was increasing domestication of animals, and pottery and weaving were practised. Neolithic ideas, although originating in the Mediterranean, seem to have reached this part of the country with people from the south west of England. These people were dark haired and in spite of the intensive ploughing of this area ever since, there are still many traces of their occupation. Large areas of forest were cleared, trackways and ditched camps constructed; the nearest being on the Trundle, three miles north west of Boxgrove. Flint was mined extensively, with the nearest site just outside the parish, at Long Down, Eartham. It is possible there were settlements along the Downs every four kilometres, mainly hamlets but some

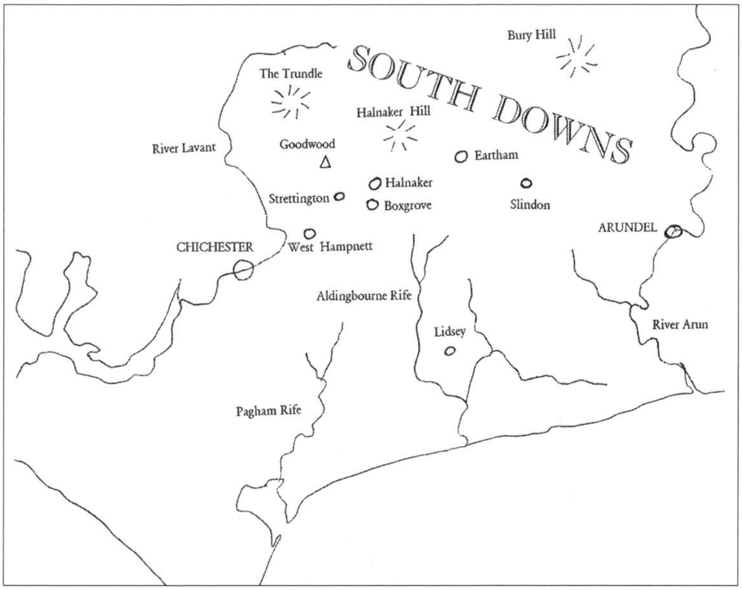

Figure 6. Significant sites near Boxgrove during the Neolithic and Iron ages.

larger villages. These people buried their dead in burial mounds or barrows: initially long barrows with multiple burials but later oval or round barrows for individuals. On Halnaker Hill there are round and oval barrows and a small but significant ditch and bank enclosure investigated by Owen Bedwin in1981-83. Firm dating evidence for the main enclosure is lacking; it could be as early as Neolithic but the surrounding field banks and barrows are of late Bronze age / early Iron age date. It has been suggested that a fairly settled economy had developed by about 3800 B.C., but before the millennium had passed the forests were regenerating, and the population shrinking as the expansion could not be sustained.

Over the next 1000 years the population fluctuated, perhaps as climate changes affected prosperity but by 2800 B.C., when Stonehenge was under construction about 60 miles to the west, late Neolithic society must have been highly organised to undertake such an immense public works. After a longish period of decline, new ideas from the Continent heralded the Bronze age. Immigrants from Europe brought metal working methods that had been developed in the Middle East. By adding tin from the Cornish mines to copper, the harder alloy, bronze, could be cast into axes, swords and armour. These 'Beaker Folk', so called because of the flat bottomed pottery they introduced, have left the bronze hoard found at Westhampnett and axes and spearheads at Bognor. Bronze was still rare and precious and flint tools continued in use and have been found together with loom weights and pottery in excavations at Ounces Barn in Boxgrove.

The Bronze Age extended for more than a millennium from about 2000-700 B.C.. During this period there were advances and setbacks. The weather became colder and drier and settlements moved from the Downs onto the Weald whilst the Downs were used for burials. Individuals were now cremated and their ashes buried in small round barrows together with their chattels as evidenced by the five bell barrows 'The Devils Jumps' eight miles north-west at Treyford.

A word should be said about the coastline. Although Boxgrove is now about 5 miles from the sea, it is certain that the coast has moved over the centuries. From a study of the soils of the coastal plain, it has been suggested that the shallow valley of the Aldingbourne Rife was, even into Saxon times, a navigable tidal estuary, of which the northern end would have been within half a mile of the parish. Much of the low lying land was marsh, or water-meadow, with a few island farms. This is borne out by such place names as Lidsey, 'Ludd's island'. Boxgrove, set between the sea and the Downs, was an ideal place to live.

After about 1500 B.C., it would seem there was a general trend to expansion of settlements and planned field systems. Many linear banks and ditches were dug to enclose grazing lands. We should imagine, perhaps, a ranch-type landscape with some villages in the river valleys and on the coastal plain.

With the next climate change, back to a warmer and wetter style, came the Celts from what is now France and Germany. No sudden invasion but a gradual infiltration of new ideas and settlers. From about 800 B.C. onwards, iron became the dominant tool material and farming even more intensive to support the ever-growing population. More land was cleared, so much so that a serious timber shortage has been suggested and the possibility that there was less woodland at the time of the Roman invasion than at the present. Iron ore was widely available whereas copper and tin were scarce. But iron working required a different

Figure 7. 'The Trundle', an Iron Age fort on the Downs above Goodwood. This aerial photograph reveals the concentric rings of an earlier Neolithic fortification.

technique using charcoal to produce the higher temperatures needed for smelting. Both oak charcoal and iron ore were readily available in the Wealden Forest and iron soon superseded other materials for tools and weapons. The Celts were a warlike people and much inter-tribal fighting is indicated by the size and strength of the hill-top forts of the 3rd. century B.C. The fort on Halnaker Hill was still in use but the most heavily fortified site in the region was on The Trundle surrounding the original Neolithic ditched camp. Field systems were extended, and a new feature appears, grain drying kilns. These would enable parched grain to be stored in quantity. There also seems to have been considerable trade with the Continent as evidenced by the broken amphorae that have been found, some originating in Spain and some from Italy which probably contained olive oil and wine.

In about 75 B.C., The first real invasion of southern England took place. The Belgae came into Kent and Essex, probably sending refugees into Sussex. Soon after, they had a settlement in Hampshire and expanded east into the Manhood peninsula. We are now at the opening of recorded history. The leader of this advance was Commius, a chief of the Atrebates, who had already been in Britain before Julius Caesar's Kentish landings in 55 B.C.. Boxgrove was certainly within his 'kingdom' as the great 10 km. earthworks, the Chichester Dykes, come through Halnaker. His centre was probably at Chichester or just to the south of it. Historians now record the beginnings of real kingdoms, with powerful rulers minting their own coins, controlling trade and industry, and raising substantial armies. From their lands, the outlines of later shires and even parishes begin to form as defined economic and political territories.

However, the overall picture was too fragmented for stability. The Romans when they came in force in 43 A.D. found an over-exploited landscape, everywhere cultivated and grazed, almost on the verge of a major social and technological collapse. Boxgrove's position, just on the edge of the Atrebates territory, with rich farmland connecting the gentle slopes of the Downs to the sea-marshes, and with trackways both along the coast and inland, may well have seen much lively action all around but was itself little altered.

BOXGROVE IN ROMAN AND SAXON TIMES

This area of Sussex seems to have played a significant but quiet part in the invasion and conquest of Britain by Claudius in A.D. 43. It was at that time ruled by Verica, who had fled to Rome seeking military aid against his northern neighbours, the Catuvellani, who were trying to expand. However it is probable that there was no fighting here at all for within a very short time the area is

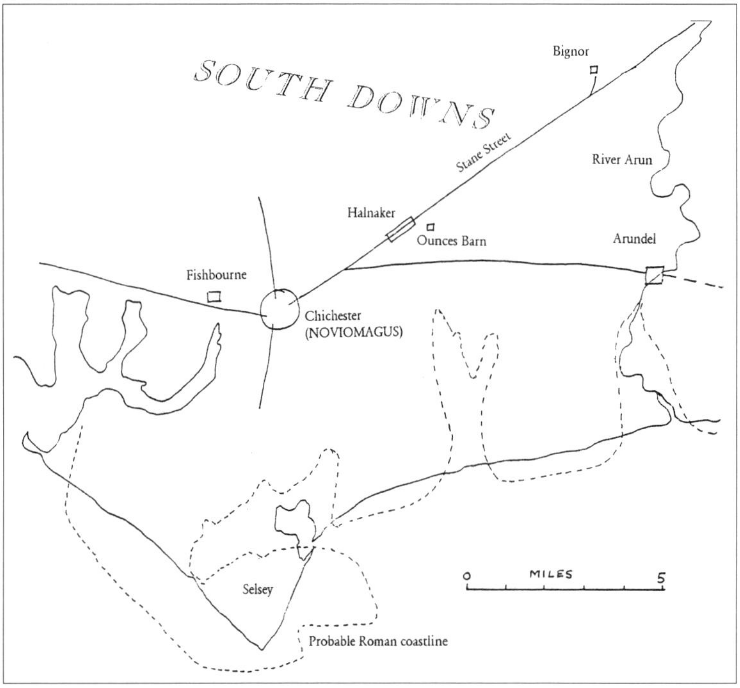

Figure 8. The coastline near Chichester as it probably existed when the Roman Palace at Fishbourne was built about 75 A.D.

referred to in Roman documents as Regnus (the Kingdom); Cogidubnus is the client king and Chichester town, Noviomagus (New Market) is flourishing. The early supply base at Fishbourne had been rebuilt as a palace or at least a major administrative centre before the end of the first century and Chichester's amphitheatre for large scale public entertainment was in place by A.D. 90.

For Boxgrove itself, there is no evidence yet of palaces, or even villas. The site at the end of the Chichester dykes where Ounces Barn now stands has provided much material from the late Iron Age right through to the fourth century A.D. with a peak of activity in the first 150 years. It would appear to have been a substantial farm. Since the town of Chichester is so close, it is possible that no villas were built here but that the existing Iron Age farms were remodelled on Roman lines. Town merchants often owned small country properties near their place of work; the rich soil and smooth south facing slopes of the Downs would have been very attractive.

It has been suggested that most of the large landowners, particularly in the south-east of Britain, were native born British. With a slightly warmer and drier climate than now, and the growing population to feed, agriculture flourished. By the late third century heavier ploughs were in use and many drainage schemes had been inaugurated so that clay soils could be worked. Crop rotation and manuring were well known and a wide range of foods grown. Pollen analysis confirms the growing of wheat, barley, rye, oats, hemp, flax, peas and beans. With the Roman preference for beef more cattle joined the sheep and pigs in the stockyards, providing milk, wool and hides. There would be plenty of surpluses for trade both at home and to the Continent. Although the Roman period is quite short, compared to the Bronze or Iron ages, the agricultural improvements, a stable government and the empire-wide economic sphere led quickly to a very large population, certainly much higher than at Domesday.

Roman coins and scattered pottery fragments have been found throughout the parish but, because of the continuous agriculture and rebuilding of houses through to the present day, no major centres have been located or excavated here. There is aerial photographic evidence for various sites: a farming complex on the slopes of the Downs below Hat Hill, an extensive field system on Halnaker Hill, a farmstead in Selhurst Park, where the arm of a Roman statue was found by chance in 1973, another set of enclosures, assumed to be Romano-British, to the north east of Warehead Farm, and a single cremation urn in a field behind the Priory.

Site investigation in 1991, prior to the construction of the major road junction of the A259 and A27 near Strettington on the western edge of the parish, revealed a wealth of archaeological material. The site, about 9000 square metres, centred on a small hillock rising about six metres above the surrounding plain, showed occupation and use from early Mesolithic times. The most important feature was a late Iron Age cemetery with over 170 burials, said to be the largest yet excavated in Britain. Most were cremated remains in shallow circular graves, buried with up to seven pottery vessels in each. Frequently one of these pots was a pedestal urn of the type known as Aylesford wheel- thrown, in use from 60-10 B.C.. There were also features containing burnt wood, mainly oak and hazel, interpreted as the remains of funeral pyres.

On the eastern side were five nearly rectangular enclosures, marked by ditches. One had a number of grave-like features, but no human remains; another enclosed a four post structure with a cremation burial in an urn at its centre. All were surrounded by a number of irregular features filled with what are thought to be the remains of pyres.

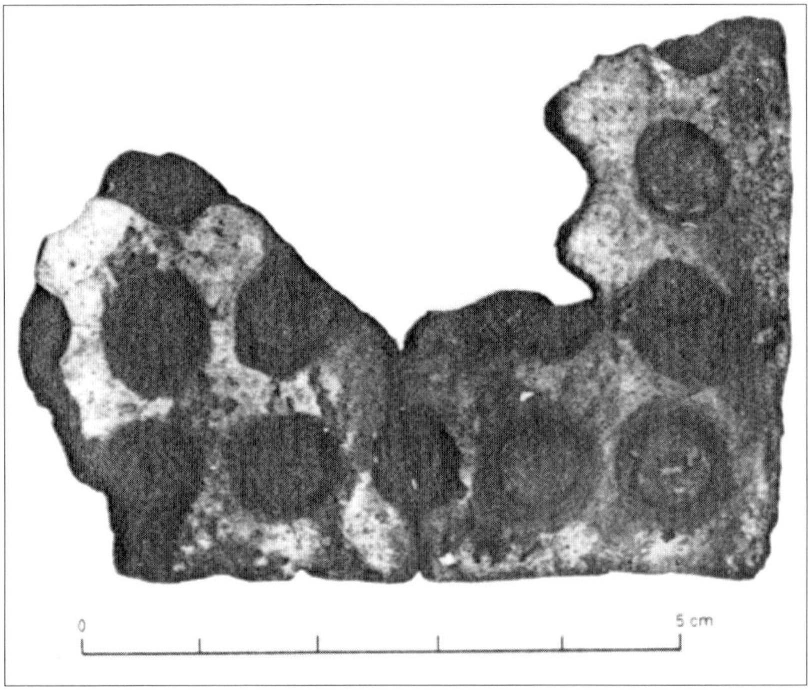

Figure 9. Clay moulds for producing gold coin blanks found amongst Roman material at Boxgrove

As well as this cemetery, a second smaller and later cemetery in the same general area was also excavated. Here most of the cremation urns were based on pottery forms which went out of use by A.D. 70, although there was one grave where a second century beaker was found. The pottery was mainly locally made but with a little Samian ware and some Lyons colour-coated vessels. This cemetery contained about forty burials in total and the grave goods included two early glass vessels and a copper alloy mirror as well as the pottery. Because of the quantity of ceramic building material, including roof, floor and flue tiles found in the immediate area, the excavators suggested the presence of 'a substantial Romano-British settlement.'

The most visible Roman feature in the parish is Stane Street, now the main road from Chichester to Petworth through Halnaker. (See II in colour section) It ran straight from the Roman East Gate of Chichester to the first posting station at Hardham near Pulborough; there it crossed the river Arun and then headed straight for London. Although constructed as a military road it was never used as such because peace in the kingdom of the Regni had already been achieved by the time it was completed. Its main use was probably for the distribution of corn from the rich lands of Sussex towards London to feed the armies further north. Because the road was intended for rapid movements of marching men and pack animals it took a direct route up steep inclines. Later civilian wheeled traffic often diverted from the Roman road to avoid these hills as at Halnaker. The road was constructed on a cleared strip of land about 80 - 90 feet wide; the roadway itself or *agger* varying from 20 - 30 feet wide. This was built up in layers of rammed chalk and flint with layers of smaller flints and gravel towards the top. Further north on Stane Street other materials were used, notably slag from iron workings in the Weald. The built-up part of the road was about two feet thick tapering away to the sides. At Westhampnett a section was excavated fully in 1937 where two drainage ditches were found at either edge of the 90 foot wide cleared area. A well preserved section can still be seen at Eartham just east of the parish.

Strangely there are no references to Stane Street in Roman records and it seems that in peacetime a more useful route north from Chichester was via Silchester into the upper Thames valley. The name 'Stane Street' first occurs in documents in 1279 in the Saxon form *Stanstret* (Stone road) but, although the road was abandoned as a through route, sections were incorporated into the modern road system.

Throughout the period of Roman influence, this area experienced none of the major military campaigns which took place in the north of England or Wales. The early revolt of Boudicca cannot have had much effect here. The sense of prosperity and calm under the Pax Romana must have been considerable. The good roads to London and along the coast made travel easy; the harbours gave ready commercial outlets to our neighbours in Gaul who spoke both the Celtic speech of Sussex and Latin. There would have been less sense of division than there is today.

The first hint of problems comes from the end of the third century, with the building of the Saxon Shore Forts and the strengthening of Chichester's city defences against sea raiders. Boxgrove would have been called upon for food supplies and perhaps manpower. By now, Britain was an almost self-sufficient province of the doomed Roman Empire. Large numbers of mercenaries had been settled here; it is very probable that Sussex had its share of them for the defence of the shore. But between 400 and 410 A.D. nearly all the regular legions and coastal garrisons were withdrawn and in the Anglo-Saxon Chronicle, unfortunately not always the most reliable source, is the first record in 477, now corrected to 457 A.D., of a Saxon landing in Britain, most probably in East Sussex.

However, many historians now believe in a much more gradual settlement than a general invasion. Some villas had been abandoned in the late fourth century and Saxon settlers were taking over lands from 350 A.D. onwards. Many town dwellers and large villa owners moved west or over the Channel; Roman society gently collapsed. We have no direct evidence of life in Boxgrove at this time. It is truly the beginning of the Dark Ages. The nearest hint of growing Saxon influence is in some place names - Oving for example: the ending 'ing' being widely recognised as an indicator of early Saxon settlement. However, the land would have been too fertile to be allowed to go to waste, and Saxon villages with large communal fields must have been planted here.

Boxgrove now becomes part of the kingdom of the South Saxons. The Wealden forest is an effective barrier to the north; Stane Street has been abandoned and all Sussex is very much isolated. The kingdom of Kent is to the east, that of the West Saxons in Hampshire and Dorset with the Jutish lands of the Meon Valley and Southampton in between. Chichester town appears to have been almost deserted until the ninth century when it began to revive.

Christianity came again to Sussex by the preaching of Saint Wilfrid, the exiled Bishop of York. In 681, some eight years or more after Kent had been converted, king Aethelwalh gave Wilfrid land on Selsey, described by Bede as 'a place surrounded by the sea on all sides except to the west where there is an approach about a sling's cast in width'. Shortly afterwards Caedwalla, king of the West Saxons (Wessex) invaded, and killed Aethelwalh, but although a pagan, he allowed the Christian church to continue. In 685 he is reported to have made a pilgrimage to Rome to be baptised and to die there. He achieved both ends. He is significant to Boxgrove in that a charter survives, drawn up by him to confirm the lands given to Wilfrid, which actually delineates the boundaries of Tangmere. This is the earliest written piece of history relating directly to this area. It is written mainly in Latin but with Saxon names. It begins, after a lengthy preamble: '*Sed et hi sunt termini pertinentibus a.d. tang mere. primitus of hleap mere per viam puplicam a.d. terram heantunensem a.d. angulum circianum. inde in locum horsa gehaeg et sic ubi dicitur hean erse. hinc a.d. aelrithe . . .* '

'These are the bounds belonging to Tangmere. Firstly from Leapmares along the highway to the Easthampnett land, to the bend, thence to the horse paddock, thus to the place called the high stubble, thence to the eel brook . . . '

The translator adds the following notes:

> *Viam puplicam* - the public road, probably maintained by the villagers and not the local landowners; most probably the original Chichester to Arundel road.
>
> *terram heantunensem* - the land of (East)hampnett, with a medial n for the Old English dative case.
>
> *hean tune* - at the high farm (no mention of East).
>
> *horsa gehaeg* - a field known as Horsehaie is listed in a deed of Boxgrove Priory, c.1200, in the Boxgrove Chartulary. (Sussex Record Soc. Vol.59)
>
> *ael rithe* - the eel stream, most probably Aldingbourne Rife, also the boundary of Boxgrove Parish.

Throughout this period, there were a succession of 'kings', perhaps little more than powerful warlords with an area of influence, but gradually controlling a larger area. By the middle of the ninth century, however, a new threat emerged, Danish raiding parties. It is unlikely that this area escaped totally unharmed, although the main Viking invasions were in the north and the east. Kent was plundered and occupied in 851. By 870 only Wessex was left unconquered. This is the time of Alfred the Great. Chichester was one of the five 'burhs' or fortified garrison towns in Sussex, and the surrounding area looked to it for help. There was a major Viking raid on Chichester in 895, repulsed with great loss to the Danes of men and ships, but the terror kept returning, recorded in the Anglo-Saxon Chronicle for 994 and again in 1000, when a great battle was fought on Bury Hill, on the Downs just to the north. At last in 1016 there was a brief peace. King Canute, although a Dane, was chosen by the Saxon lords as king.

At this time two territorial divisions emerged as important units of local administration: the hundred and the parish. Boxgrove parish in the hundred of Box may well have begun to acknowledge its present boundaries by the mid tenth century. The hundred was the court of justice equivalent to at least the modern County Court and also dealt with many other matters including highways and policing. The parishes were also being created as the units of church administration, with more churches being built as learning spread and more priests were ordained.

Boxgrove is known to have had a Saxon church; indeed it may have been a minster, a large establishment with several clergy to serve a wider area. A section of masonry wall of Saxon style was exposed in 1998 during remedial work on the Priory underneath the present ruined nave. Its exact date is not known but other Saxon work in our local churches, notably at Westhampnett, dates from the first part of the eleventh century just before the Norman Conquest. It is suggested that a ready supply of wood had been available for centuries, but perhaps its vulnerability to fire lead to a wider use of stone. Even then many of the surviving stone buildings show evidence of wooden building styles translated or copied in stone.

Figure 10. Reconstruction of a 12th Century Cottage based on archeological evidence from Hangleton. Earlier cottages were probably timber framed.

It is to this period also that we probably owe the development of the village street, with a group of families all living together rather than scattered in hamlets. Obviously little evidence remains, but the somewhat straggling and random alignments of houses in close proximity in Boxgrove and Halnaker may well reflect continuity back to Saxon times. How large were these settlements? Only twenty years after the Norman Conquest, in 1086, the Domesday survey of the whole country was carried out, so a fairly clear picture can be constructed for the end of Saxon Sussex.

The largest single group of inhabitants is named *villani* or villagers. These had a share in the common fields and owed various services and dues to the feudal lord. The size of their holdings ranged from seven to thirty acres. Below them are the bordars, then the cottars, with little land, maintaining themselves by working for their neighbours. At the bottom of the scale are the serfs, mostly household servants, very few in rural Sussex. In Domesday, Boxgrove, Halnaker and East Hampnett all belong to 'William from the Earl' (Roger of Montgomery who held the combined rapes of Chichester and Arundel, in all about 83 manors{Rape being a term unique to Sussex for a group of hundreds assigned to one lord}). In two parts there are sub-tenants; Boxgrove itself having Humphrey, William, Nigel and the clergy of the church; Hampnett (note that 'east' is not used) is held by Nigel, possibly the same man as held the part of Boxgrove. Halnaker is the largest and most valuable holding: nine hides (each about one hundred and twenty acres according to a popular reckoning), land for five ploughs, seventeen villagers and twelve cottagers, eight acres of meadow, woodland for nine pigs (quite small compared to other Sussex entries) ,and income of three burgesses in Chichester at five shillings. Total value before 1066: £4, now 100 shillings (that is in 1086).

Boxgrove (six hides) has 1 villager and 12 cottagers, and is valued at forty shillings. Hampnett (7 hides) has eight villagers and eleven cottagers with three acres of meadow, all valued at 60s before 1066, now 50s. The population of Sussex actually listed in Domesday is between ten and eleven thousand. This refers to heads of households only, so a total population might be sixty to seventy thousand. With this same reckoning applied to Boxgrove, Halnaker and Hampnett we get a figure of around three and four hundred people.

Figure 11. Reconstruction of the main room and open hearth of a cottage at Hangleton, c. 12th Century.

Life in a rural community at this time probably followed a similar pattern throughout southern England. Arable land was divided into long narrow strips to aid the demarcation of ownership and the rotation of crops; perhaps wheat, barley, peas, beans or fallow pasture. The strips made up open fields and were bounded by ploughed furrows which also acted as open drainage. At Boxgrove, land was owned by the feudal lord at Halnaker or by the Priory, with some common land subdivided and worked by the villagers. Most of the population were dependent labourers, bound in service to their feudal lord, required to work his land when called upon, unable to leave their holdings and even requiring his consent to the marriages of their children. They would have lived in timber-framed cottages with clay, dung and wattle walls, earth floors with an open hearth and a thatched roof. They ploughed with oxen, kept pigs, chickens and in this area sheep, for English wool was a high quality tradeable product. Rabbits and wild birds were also trapped for the pot, but life was physically very hard with labour from dawn to dusk in all weathers giving a short life expectancy. This was the pattern of life in the parish in early Norman England.

PLACENAMES IN THE PARISH OF BOXGROVE

BOXGROVE - The earliest record of this spelling is 1337; previous versions being Bosegrave 1228, Boxgrava 1225, and Bosgrave in Domesday Book. In 1836 the Revd. Edward Turner wrote 'The origin of the name is involved in some obscurity.' Its derivation remains uncertain. There are two main contenders from Anglo-Saxon English : *græf*, a grave, trench or pit and *graf*, a grove or thicket. Both these are claimed fairly indiscriminately as the source for other places ending in -grove. The hundred in which the parish is situated is listed in Domesday as Bosgrave, so it is said that this is the village near the græf or ditch. This seems plausible as we have the end of the massive Chichester Dykes system at Halnaker. However the seal of Boxgrove Priory, dating from the late thirteenth century, has the rhyming inscription:

Dicitur ex ligno viridi Boxgravia digno
nomine nam crescit virtutibus atque virescit

which has been translated as 'Boxgrove is appropriately named after the green tree, for it grows and flourishes with virtues.' It should be noted however that there are no box trees near, and no evidence that there have ever been!

HALNAKER- This settlement has had an amazing number of variant spellings of its name: Helneche in Domesday, Hannac 1105, Hennac 1185, Halfnaked 1200's to 1400's, Hanycarr 1605, Hanekar 1650. The Oxford Dictionary of English Place-names derives it from the Anglo-Saxon *Healfanæcer* meaning half a strip of ploughed land. Mawer and Stenton in 'The Place-names of Sussex', suggest that the corruption of the English name to *Hannac* is a good example of the French language influence of an important Norman feudal centre.

CROCKERHILL- This name was in use in 1220 denoting the place where the maker of crocks (the potter) lived.

SEABEACH- This has no connection, regrettably, with the sea or beaches, although in prehistoric times the sea was there! It derives from either 'Seven Beech trees' or more likely 'Seofa's valley'.(*beche* - a stream or valley.)

STRETTINGTON- The *tun* or settlement of the dwellers by the street (Stane Street). Saxon *Stræt-tun* or as in Domesday 'Stratone'. Other later versions have been Strethamton 1288 and even Estretementona 1332.

GOODWOOD- 1200 Godinawuda and 1225 Godivewod. Almost certainly from 'Godgiefu's wood'. This was a fairly common Saxon woman's name usually Latinised as Godiva.

EASTHAMPNETT- The 'East' came later. From the Saxon *Hean tun* (at the high settlement), with the diminutive French ending 'et' added. There was an East- in 1275 and West- in 1317.

WAREHEAD- Derivation unknown , but it was being named as such by 1753.

TEMPLE BAR- Elsewhere in the country, such a name is always associated with the Knights Templar; however the nearest known Templar property would seem to be at Sompting.

I. An artist's impression of the Boxgrove area as it may have appeared 500,000 years ago.

II. Stane Street, near Eartham, showing the raised and cambered road surface.

III. The ruins of the old fortified manor of Halnaker House as seen from the air in 1995.

IV. Halnaker Mill.

V. The ceiling of the Priory nave painted by Lambert Barnard around 1520.

VI. Detail of the Priory ceiling above the altar showing the heraldic shields and flower design.

VII. The Chantry Chapel of Thomas De La Warr. When it was built in 1532 an aisle pillar had to be removed to accommodate it.

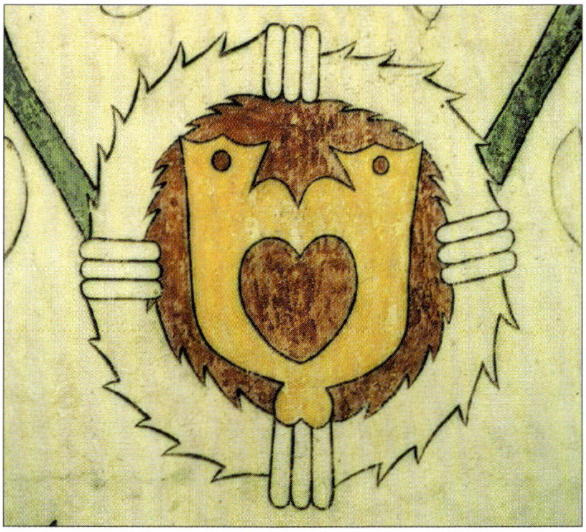

VIII. The heraldic badge of the De La Warr family. Sir Roger De La Warr, at the Battle of Poitiers 1356, took the French king John prisoner on the field and added this badge to the coat of arms of his ancestors. The family was proud of this badge and it is much in evidence in the Priory. It represents the metal tip of a scabbard and is called a crampet in heraldry. Sometimes it is referred to as a 'crampe or', and sometimes a chape.

IX. The two heads above the left and right lancets in the east window. They represent William d'Aubigny, Earl of Arundel and his wife, Adeliza, widow of Henry I, who is wearing a crown. William d'Aubigny was the brother-in-law of Robert de la Haye, Lord of Halnaker, and together they were founders of Boxgrove priory.

X. The eight-faced boss. At one of the intersections of the ribbed vaulting of the ceiling, is an interesting boss. It depicts eight faces, each one has a mouth and nose, but there are only eight eyes. Yet it appears as if each face has two eyes. It is a good example of a 'trompe-l'oeil', a deception of the eye by an artistic trick.

XI. In the south transept there is a statue of St. Blaise, who with the Virgin Mary, is the patron of the Priory. He was Bishop of Sebaste in Cappadocia in modern Turkey and he was martyred in the fourth century. His statue, which is modern, is in a niche above the altar in his chapel. This is the work of Professor Tristram of the Royal College of Art.

XII. Henry VIII 1491-1547 by an unknown artist.

XIII. Edward VI 1537-1553 by an unknown artist.

XIV. Cardinal Wolsey 1475-1530 by an unknown artist.

XV. Thomas Cromwell, First Earl of Essex 1485-1540.
After Hans Holbein.

XVI. Sir Antony Browne First Viscount Montague who entertained Edward VI at Cowdray Park in 1552 during the royal progress through Sussex.

XVII. Halnaker Park in 1629. Goodwood Ms. E4981. Reproduced by Courtesy of the Directors of the Goodwood Estate Company Limited and acknowledgments to the West Sussex Record Office and the County Archivist.

XVIII. The Morley coat of arms. The leopard's head with fleur-de-lis was an emblem of the Cantiloupe family and the mullets which decorated the chevrons were from crests of the Bonville and St. John families. Connections dating back to the Norman nobles who originally built Halnaker House.

XIX. 3rd Duke of Richmond by Reynolds. Reproduced by kind permission of the Trustees of the Goodwood Collection.

XX. The grandstand at Goodwood in 1833. Reproduced by kind permission of the Trustees of the Goodwood Collection.

XXI. The Lawn at Goodwood in 1886. Reproduced by kind permission of the Trustees of the Goodwood Collection.

XXII. 3rd Duke of Richmond with the Charlton Hunt by George Stubbs c. 1770. Reproduced by kind permission of the Trustees of the Goodwood Collection.

XXIII. Cricket in Marylebone Fields by Francis Hayman (c. 1743-7). At that time the stumps were two forked sticks with a bail resting across the forks; bowling was underarm, bats were curved and the scorers notched sticks to record runs.

XXIV. The Boxgove 'Village Store' in the 1990s. A study in watercolour by David Goodman.

XXV. The Anglesey Arms, Halnaker in the 1990s. A study in watercolour by David Goodman.

XXVI. Aerial view of Boxgrove in 1998.

THE COMING OF THE NORMANS

When Duke William of Normandy was crowned King of England in Westminster Abbey on Christmas Day 1066, many of the knights present on that occasion had landed with him at Pevensey in September and fought with him at the Battle of Hastings on 14th October. After the defeat of Harold, Earl of Wessex, these knights went on to collect their rewards in the form of grants of land throughout the conquered kingdom. Some of them were given land in West Sussex, and these are the ones who concern us here in Boxgrove.

Figure 12. The Bayeux Tapestry shows William (carrying a mace) leading his knights into battle

These knights undoubtedly believed that they had a right to conquered lands. They had fought with William under a banner blessed by Pope Alexander II. Because the Normans enforced clerical celibacy and at least paid lip service in opposing clerical simony - the buying and selling of ecclesiastical offices or preferment - the Pope was leniently disposed towards the invasion. Duke William had also persuaded Alexander, before he set sail for England, that Harold had agreed to his accession to the English throne after the death of Edward the Confessor, and had subsequently reneged on his promise, hence incurring the stigma of 'oath breaker'.

Figure 13. Map showing Boxgrove and Lessay

William, as Duke of Normandy, had sponsored the creation of new monastic foundations in his dukedom and had encouraged his nobles to do likewise, with such success that it is estimated that there were over twenty six monasteries in his domain before he invaded England. William always considered himself as a champion of religious reform and again was able to convince the Pope that one of his chief reasons for invading England was to set about reforming the Anglo-Saxon church.

Thus many of William's followers, knowing that they had the support and blessing of the Pope, fought with a moral fervour and looked forward to obtaining their rewards. After the Anglo-Saxons were pacified, and that took longer than expected, many of these nobles did receive their rewards. Some of them gained lands and manors in West Sussex. The three Norman families connected with Boxgrove sprang from villages in the Cherbourg peninsular in Normandy, La Haye du Puits, St Martin d'Aubigny and St John-le-Thomas. William d'Aubigny became Earl of Arundel in the reign of Henry 1st, and Robert de la Haye, grandson of Tirstin Haldup, the first Lord de la Haye, who was Senescal of Count Robert of Montain, received from the King, in 1105 in return for his services, the honor of Halnaker which included Boxgrove, Walberton, Barnham, East and West Hampnett, Birdham and other lands. This honor, at the time of Domesday 1086, was held by one William, undertenant of Earl Roger Montgomery, Lord of the Rape of Arundel, who however forfeited his lands in 1102. It was this Robert de la Haye who founded the Priory at Boxgrove, together with William d'Aubigny, his overlord, whose sister he married in 1108. They agreed to give their local abbey in Normandy, the Abbey of Lessay, a gift of property in England. The Benedictine Abbey of Lessay was of special significance to Robert de la Haye because the abbey had been founded by his grandfather, Tirstin Haldup in 1056, as a daughterhouse of the great monastery of Bec in Normandy.

Figure 14. L' Abbaye de Lessay in Normandy, mother house of Boxgrove priory

Baron Robert built his principal residence at Halnaker, but today all that remains of this house is just a shell. Another, modern house has been built on the site. But the ruins of the old fortified manor house, it was never a castle, still reflect some of its former glory. The ruins that we see today originated mainly in the fourteenth century (See III in colour section) but there are traces of earlier work and later, there was extensive rebuilding when the house was owned by Lord De La Warr in the sixteenth century. It was in 1105 that Robert de la Haye, together with his brother-in-law William d'Aubigny decided to build a Priory on the site of the old Saxon church of St Mary. In the Boxgrove Chartulary, a collection of documents relating to the Priory and it's subsequent expansion under the descendants of Robert de la Haye through grants of land and other benefactions, there is a record of the original grant of land to the monks of Lessay.

'Robert Hay, (de Haia) son of Ranulph, the Senescal of Robert Count of Montain, nephew of Eudo, the steward (dapifer) of King William I, notifying that in the year 1105, Henry being King of England, with his wife Matilda, he has given to the Abbey of the Holy Trinity, L'Essay, for his soul and those of King Henry and his wife, of the fee of Hannac, which that King gave to him, these churches with their lands and tithes: the church of St. Mary of Boxgrove in the diocese of Chichester, two and a half hides of land around it, and the whole tithe of that parish and of his Christmas rents there and the tithe of his wood, from pannage (pasture for pigs) and sale (salt), with firing and timber for their buildings and pannage for their swine and pasture for all their stock'.

Figure 15. The ruins of the old fortified manor of Halnaker House as seen from Halnaker park.

Robert de la Haye also gave to Lessay tithes and fees to St Peter, Westhampnett, St Leger of Hunston, Birdham, Walberton, St Mary of Barnham and other churches in the area. The Abbot of Lessay despatched three monks to Boxgrove to superintend their new property, and the building of the Priory began between 1117-1120.

The Lords of Halnaker became the patrons of the priory until the eighteenth century, except for an interval at the time of the Dissolution when the manor of Halnaker was seized by the crown. The descent of the Lords of the manor of Halnaker came through the female line. For instance, Robert de la Haye had one daughter, Cicely, who succeeded to the Manor. She married Roger St John who made extensive gifts to the Priory so as to allow an increase in the number of its monks from three to six. Her two sons, William and Robert, were also benefactors. William gave endowments to maintain thirteen monks. Later the number was increased to fifteen. Robert St John, his brother, granted land at Walberton and Barnham to support a sixteenth monk. This monk acted as chaplain at Halnaker House.

William and Robert died without issue. Their sister, Muriel, succeeded to Halnaker and married into the St John family. During the twelfth and thirteenth centuries the family of St John were owners of Halnaker and patrons of the Priory. It was through the continuous patronage of the Lords of Halnaker that the Priory was able to expand and flourish. The St Johns were succeeded by the Poynings family through the marriage of Isabel St John to Luke de Poynings. Four generations of Poynings followed. The last member was Joan who married Thomas Bonville of Shute in Devonshire in about 1394. Their son, John Bonville, born in 1413, and his second wife, Katherine Wingfield, both left interesting wills. He made his on 30 May 1494 - he died in 1495 - when he was eighty one years old. In it he left six shillings and eight pence to John Preston, 'chapleyne at Halfnaked'. He also left a Breviary and Processional, that is a Directory of the Ritual of Processions. It was to be fastened with a 'chayne of iron' to the lectern.

Katherine Bonville made her will in 1497. In it she said she wanted to be buried in Boxgrove Church and asked that her husband's body be brought back from Shute to lie with her. She left three shillings and four pence to the reparations of the cathedral church of Chichester. To the Priory of Boxgrove she left fifty one shillings to buy them some 'blue frontelles' for the high altar to match their blue vestments which were given to them by her husband and herself. To the Prior she left 'the best horse of my stables' and a cup of silver with a covering for it known as Bishop Lacey's cup. Also a powder box of silver and a little silver goblet.

In 1495 Elizabeth, the daughter of Sir John Bonville and Katherine Wingfield, married Sir Thomas West, the ninth Lord De La Warr. He proved to be one of the main benefactors of the Priory, saving it for posterity at the time of the Dissolution.

Thus the Norman knights who came over with Duke William in 1066, the St John family, the Poynings, and the Bonvilles, settled down in the honor of Halnaker and became generous patrons of the Priory. Without their patronage it is doubtful whether the Priory could have flourished and survived as it did until the years of the Reformation. It is a good example of a Manor and a Monastery working together and sharing a common prosperity, and in 1536, a common fate. Their family crests and coats of arms can be seen all over the Priory, most notably on the painted ceilings and carved on the Chantry chapel, memorials of the Priory's generous benefactors.

A HOLY RELIC AT HALNAKER

Luke de Ponynges, Lord of Halnaker and patron of Boxgrove Priory died in 1375. In his will which was proved at Southward on 4 July 1376 he gave a set of red vestments for the use of the high altar at Boxgrove and £40 in silver towards the fabric of the same church. J.L. André writing in the Sussex Archaeological Collections describes how he also bequeathed to the Cathedral Church of St Paul's, London, the head of St Gamaliel together with the sum of £15 'towards the ornamentation of the said head'. This curious bequest provokes a number of questions. How did this saintly relic arrive at Boxgrove and what happened to it? There is little hard fact available but there are a few clues and it may be interesting to speculate.

St Gamaliel was the Pharisee and doctor of law at whose feet St Paul was brought up. According to legend his remains were discovered in 415 A.D. about 20 miles from Jerusalem, buried beside those of St Stephen, the first Christian martyr. Bede records the discovery of these relics and reports that those of St Stephen were quickly dispersed with great devotion and brought to western Europe by Orosius. It is probable that the remains of St Gamaliel were treated with similar veneration and also taken to Europe at the same time.

We know that in 415 A.D., Orosius was sent by St Augustine of Hippo to St Jerome in Palestine. Orosius was a young Spanish monk who had fled his home in the face of vandal invasions and who became a disciple of Augustine. He was

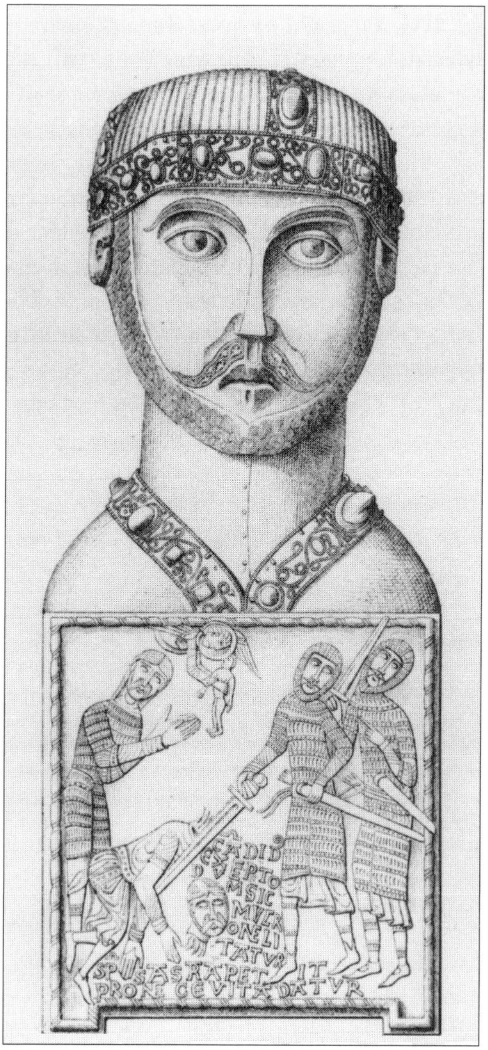

Figure 16. Reliquary of St Candide preserved in Switzerland. The head of St Gamaliel was probably mounted and ornamented in a similar way.

later to become an important historian of the early Christian church. Orosius had been sent to Jerome to assist in a heresy indictment against Pelagius at a Jerusalem synod in 415. Being at hand when the sepulchre of the saints was discovered, it appears that their relics returned with him to Augustine as reported by Bede.

Throughout the Dark and Middle Ages holy relics were objects of deep veneration. They were carefully preserved in cathedrals and churches throughout Christendom and the more famous attracted many pilgrims who brought offerings to their shrines. It seems likely that Gamaliel's skull was preserved somewhere in Western France but we have no evidence of this.

We know that in 1346 Michael de Ponynges, the elder brother of Luke de Ponynges was in France with the English army at the beginning of the Hundred Years War. 'The Acts of War of Edward III', a manuscript diary of the Crécy Campaign probably written by a member of the Black Prince's Council, describes how 'a famous and unconquered army of nobles, knights and commons and a fleet of ships terrible to both the eye and the mind of the enemy, assembled from all parts of England at Portsmouth'.

On 12 July 1346 they landed at La Hougue on the Cherbourg peninsular where the army was split into three divisions. The Black Prince led the vanguard. Amongst the nobles in the centre, led by the King were Michael Ponynges and Edward Montagu. The rearguard, under the Bishop of Durham, included the Earl of Arundel and William Cantilupe. The army, pillaging and burning as they went, sacked Barfleur and Cormolain, and entered St Lo. Caen was sacked on 27 July where 'the English eagerly returned to the work of despoiling the town, only taking jewels, clothing or precious ornaments because of the abundance'. The English fleet had followed the army along the coast burning towns and manors and more than 100 French ships. 'They found such a mass of goods sent to them that they could not transport all the spoils from Caen and elsewhere. On the 28th nothing more was done except that the countryside was set on fire all round. On the 29th, fifteen of the greatest citizens of Bayeux came to surrender that town.'

It seems clear that large quantities of captured valuables were sent back to England during the campaigns of Edward III and the Black Prince in western France. We know that Michael Ponynges fought there and it is possible that he may have acquired the skull of Gamaliel at that time from one of the religious houses overrun. Perhaps this valuable relic was then passed on to Luke de Ponynges, his younger brother, who bequeathed it to St Paul's at his death.

This relic certainly came into the possession of Old St Paul's for it is included amongst the devotional 'Reliquae' in their care described by William Dugdale in 'The History of St Paul's Cathedral in London', where it is listed as 'Item Caput S. Gamalielis auripictum, cum lapidibus circa humeros insertis'. [Head of St Gamaliel decorated with gold with precious stones inserted around the shoulders.] It appears that the money left by Luke de Poynings towards the ornamentation of the head had been well used, for the skull was now mounted in the form of a bust, probably decorated with fold leaf and with jewels around the shoulders. The subsequent fate of the head is unknown but it probable disappeared during the Reformation at the time of the ransacking of ecclesiastical buildings of their treasures.

A contemporary writer states that in September 1547 there appeared in St Paul's the Commissioners for the execution of the Edict of the Council which commanded the destruction of images in churches and ordained the discontinuance of all customs held to be superstitious. Milman in his 'Annals of St Paul's Cathedral' records that on 5 September began 'the King's visitation at Powll's (St Paul's) and all the images were pulled down.'

It seems likely that the relic of St Gamaliel was plundered of its jewels and destroyed at that time for nothing more has been heard of it.

A BENEDICTINE COMMUNITY

'In all things, therefore, let all follow the Rule as master, nor let anyone rashly depart from it.'

The three monks who came over from Lessay to supervise the building of a Priory under the patronage of Robert de la Haye and William d'Aubigny, were Benedictines, and consequently were bound by the Rule of St Benedict which was drawn up in the sixth century A.D. by the saint to serve as a guide line for monks sharing a communal life. The first task facing the monks was to provide a suitable building. They began this task between 1117 and 1120 and subsequently put in process a building project which gave employment to many local people. The technical design and oversight of the building would have been in the hands of a master builder who would have learnt his skills through working on other monasteries or cathedrals. He would have gathered a team of master craftsmen, stonemasons, quarrymen, carpenters, blacksmiths and glass-makers who would have been supported by their own assistants and apprentices. The local population would have provided the labourers as well as the services necessary to look after the needs of the monks and craftsmen; tilling the fields, looking after the sheep and other stock and making the beer, cheese and bread which formed the staple diet of the monks. As the number of monks increased from the original three to nineteen at the peak of the Priory's prosperity in the thirteenth century, due to the patronage of the Lords of the Manor of Halnaker and other patrons, so the workforce supporting the Priory

Figure 17. St Benedict, the founder of Western monasticism established the Benedictine Order about 520A.D. at Monte Cassino near Naples.

correspondingly increased to cater for their needs. Most people living in Boxgrove and Halnaker must have found work in one way or another, with the Priory, and at the Dissolution, many would lose their employment and endure considerable hardship in adapting to the new society.

The monks began to build their own church in the early years of the twelfth century together with the other buildings necessary for a monastic community. By 1160 the early stage was completed, a church, known as the monks' choir, a crossing with a low tower on top, a chapter house and a cloister. Probably the refectory and the monks' dormitory were completed at the same time.

They also built a parish church separated from the monks' choir by a screen at the east end. This church was built over the old Anglo-Saxon church which had been given to the Abbot of Lessay by Robert de la Haye and William d'Aubigny, his overlord, along with other lands and tithes in Boxgrove. In the original grant of land to the Abbot of Lessay, the Anglo-Saxon church was called the church of Saint Mary of Boxgrove. This church, with a south aisle and a north aisle which abutted onto the cloisters, together with the monks' choir, created a long, low, sturdy building in which the parishioners of Boxgrove and the monastic community worshipped in close proximity.

The twelfth century buildings were built in the sturdy Norman style with round arches and strong pillars. Some of the capitals were decorated with elegant designs. The walls would have been painted with bright pictures showing scenes from the Bible and episodes from the lives of the saints. Today, all that remains of these wall paintings is just a small patch at the west end of the present nave, near the bell rope, and a faint picture in the south transept which probably showed St George killing his dragon. Recently, whilst re-decorating the area of wall by the entrance porch, some more traces of wall paintings were discovered. Unfortunately, the English climate doesn't help the preservation of these early frescoes, but they do give us some idea of what the interior of the church looked like in Mediaeval times.

The cloisters and chapter house were also built in the early twelfth century. The cloisters were the place where, in fine weather, the monks would have exercised and worked, and was easily accessible for the daily meetings in the chapter house, where most of the monastic business was conducted. The cloister was sixty two feet by fifty eight feet, and the corbels, which carried the roofing timbers, are still there. On the upper line of the corbels rested the rafters of the lean-to roof, and the lower carried either the tie beams or diagonal braces. The cloister arcade was probably made of wood and consequently was one of the first

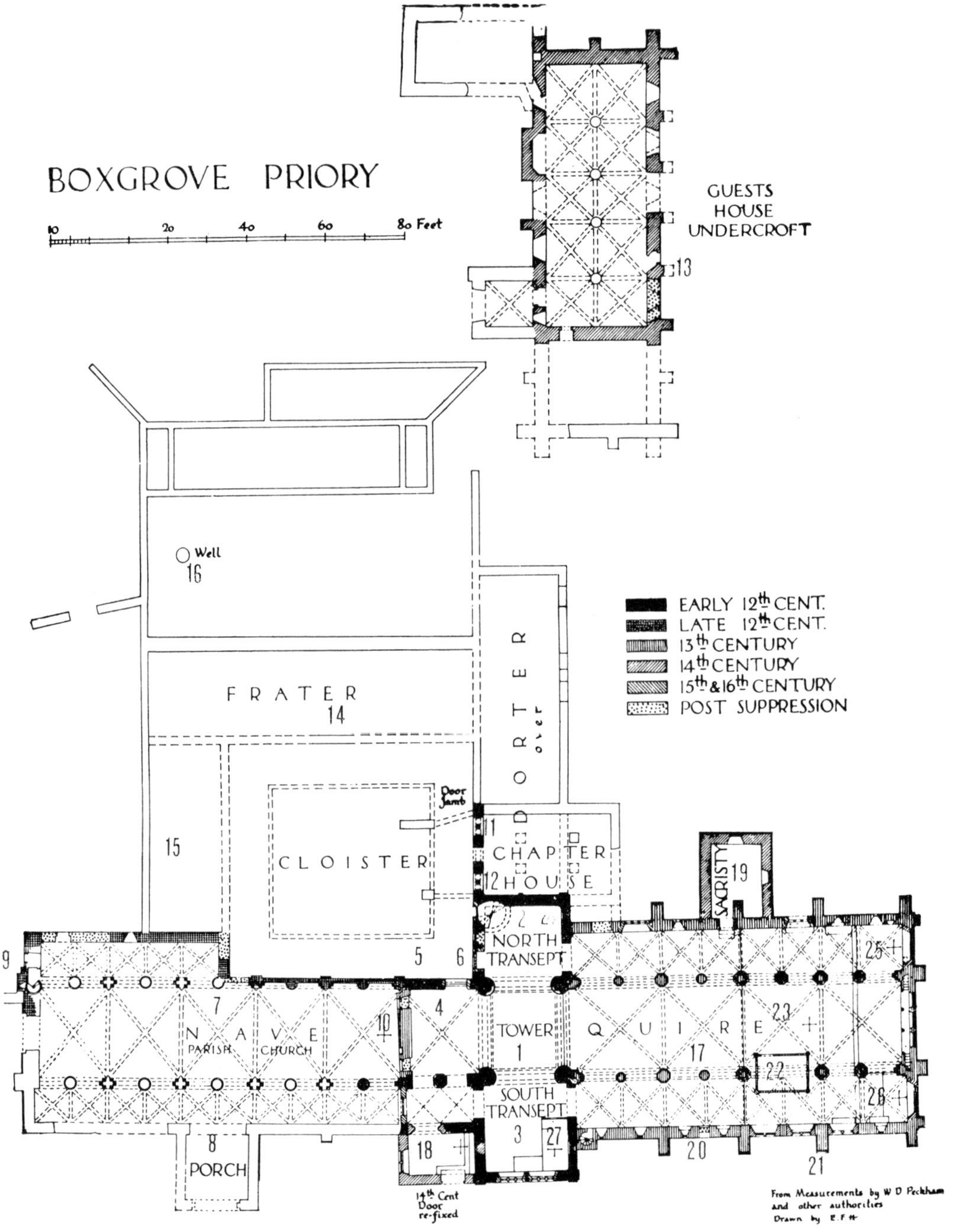

Plan reproduced by permission of the Sussex Archaeological Society and the Royal Archaeological Institute.

Figure 18. Plan of Boxgrove Priory showing periods of constuction

parts of the Priory to decay after the Dissolution.

To the north of the cloister was probably the refectory and warming room, and to the west would have been the kitchens, the brewery, and dairies, and other buildings required to provide the monks and their guests with everything they needed, in accordance with the Rule which says that all necessary things, such as water, mill, garden and various crafts, which a monastery requires, should be inside the enclosure.

In the early part of the thirteenth century, although the original Priory had barely been completed, it was decided for the greater glory of God to enlarge and heighten the building. The decision was taken to rebuild the monk's choir and transepts in the new style, increasing the height of the nave and tower and supporting the new walls by flying buttresses. This new work was finished around 1230. The transepts were probably the last thing done before the building of the Prior's house and guest house at the end of the century.

The new style made use of pointed arches, typical of Early English or Gothic architecture. It resulted in a taller, lighter building with a clerestory and larger windows which let in more light than the previous Norman ones. The choir was vaulted with four bays, eight in the aisles, creating a spacious effect. In this country this double-bay vaulting is quite rare but not uncommon on the Continent.

By the end of the thirteenth century, the parish church with the monks' Priory was a large and imposing building, lying in the heart of the village of Boxgrove. The villagers would attend their church each Sunday, of course, and there would have been an entrance porch for them on the south side of their long nave with a room above it, probably to house the priest. The parish altar would have been at the east end set between the aumbry and piscina which are still there. On either side of the altar there are low doors which would be opened for processions in which the parish took part, or when the parish priest and the monks wished to communicate with each other.

Then, at the end of the thirteenth century, the monks built the Prior's house, which today is a romantic ruin situated in a field to the north of the Priory. It was not only the place where the Prior lived and worked, but also served as a guest house for the many travellers and visitors who came to the Priory expecting hospitality. The monks were always hospitable, in accordance with the instructions of their founder, St Benedict. In chapter twenty three of the Rule he says:

'Let all guests that come be received like Christ, for he will say: I was a stranger

Figure 19. Ruins of the Prior's House and Guest House

and ye took me in. And let fitting honour be shown to all, but especially to churchmen and pilgrims. As soon, therefore, as a guest is announced, let the superior or some brethren meet him with all charitable service. And first of all let them pray together, and let them unite in the kiss of peace. This kiss of peace shall not be offered until after the prayers have been said, on account of the delusions of the devil. In the greeting of all guests, whether they be arriving or departing, let the greatest humility be shown.'

Rooms would have been set aside for these guests, and on the south side of the building there was probably a solarium where important guests would stay. On the first floor of the building above the vaulted undercroft where the kitchens were situated, and where the tiled back of the fireplace is still clearly seen, would have been the great hall where guests were entertained. There was probably a chapel on this floor for the Prior's use and for the private use of his more important guests. Above the main hall there was probably another floor where ordinary people could bed down for the night.

The guest house was set aside from the main part of the Priory so that the monks would not be disturbed by the comings and goings of these visitors, but even so, there must have been a continuous bustle taking place which would have disturbed the tranquillity of the monks' life. The monks also had a duty to receive and look after the sick in their hospital, and to provide daily alms for the poor people who came to the gate house each day to receive these alms.

There would be a porter at the gate house as the Rule stipulates, 'At the gate of the monastery let there be placed a wise old man, who understands how to give and receive a message, and whose years will keep him from leaving his post. This porter should have a room near the gate, so that those who come may always find someone to answer them. As soon as anyone knocks, or a poor man hails him, let him answer 'Deo gratias' or 'Benedic'.'

By the end of the fourteenth century, building works had mostly ceased except for a sacristy, which was added in the fifteenth century. However, various changes to the interior of the monks' choir took place, mainly due to the instructions of one of the Priory's great patrons, Thomas West, 9th Lord De La Warr, Lord of the Manor of Halnaker in the first half of the sixteenth century. There will be much more about him in a later chapter.

It was he who commissioned the local Chichester artist, Lambert Barnard, to paint the ceiling of the monks' choir around 1520 (see V in colour section). Barnard was founder of a remarkable school of early English Renaissance painters which originated from his house on the south side of East Street in Chichester. Barnard had a powerful patron in the person of Robert Sherbourne, bishop of Chichester, who spent large sums of money on beautifying the cathedral and paid for Barnard's work out of his own privy purse as there is no record of these payments in the Chapter Accounts. While he was commissioned to work for the Bishop, or anyone connected with the cathedral, he would receive for his pay, his keep and the hire of his assistant, a sum of about £14 a year, together with the cost of his colours and his gold and silver.

The ceiling of the Priory choir was decorated in the English medium of distemper, that is paint on dry plaster, and was inspired by the flowers and plants that grew in the fields and gardens all around him, for example vines, roses, pinks, honeysuckle, blackberries and fritillaries. The effect is a stunning fantasy of flowers which serves as a background for the shields and heraldic devices which decorate the ceiling (see VI in colour section). The shields are the coats of arms of the families connected with Lord De La Warr (see VIII in colour section). The heraldic devices are the insignia of his own family and the other families with which his name is linked, such as the Poynings, the St Johns, the Mortimers, the Cantilupes and the Wingfields.

The first compartment, above the present high altar, represents Thomas, eighth Lord De La Warr and his wife, Joan Mortimer. The second compartment, Thomas, ninth Lord De La Warr and his wife, Elizabeth Bonville. The third represents Katherine Wingfield, his mother and father-in-law, and the fourth compartment represents Hugh Poynings and Elizabeth Ferrers, the great grandparents of Elizabeth Bonville, wife of the ninth Lord De La Warr.

Thomas West also ordered the building of a chantry chapel in the Priory choir to serve as a tomb for himself and his wife, and where masses were to be said for the repose of their souls. To fit the chantry chapel into the arcade, the central pillar had to be removed (see VII in colour section). The chapel is lavishly adorned with charming carvings probably drawn from a French Book of Hours now in the Cathedral library. The figures reflect an interesting mixture of Gothic and Renaissance styles.

Thus from the twelfth to the sixteenth centuries, the Priory was continually being built, extended and decorated, providing continuous work for the artisans of the surrounding villages (see X in colour section). The Dissolution must have inflicted a shattering blow to the local economy.

The Boxgrove community had provided it's own Prior since it's foundation (see IX in colour section), and the Abbot of Lessay was bound not to remove him without good reason. The Prior filled vacancies in the number of monks but it was to the Abbot that they made their profession. The Abbot had the right to withdraw any monk except the sub-Prior and the cellarer. There was a certain amount of contact between Boxgrove and Lessay, and a house in Portsmouth, from which the Priory received rent, was kept available as a staging post for monks making the journey.

Gradually, as time passed, this connection with the French mother house began to fade. In 1275 the Abbot of Lessay took advantage of a vacancy and attempted to assert his rights by nominating one of his own monks, Ralph de Duno, as Prior. After consulting the community, the Bishop of Chichester refused to accept the nomination and appointed one of his own monks, Robert, to the vacancy. This dispute went on for some time, finally being taken first to the Archbishop of Canterbury and then to the Pope, Honorius IV, who gave a decision in favour of Boxgrove Priory. As a result of the matter Robert Kilwordey, Archbishop of Canterbury, made a personal visit to the Priory in 1275. He made a number of injunctions. To quote some:

> The monks were living too well and not following the dietary rules of their Order as to the consumption of meat.
>
> The monks had taken to wearing brown robes in place of the black habit

prescribed by the Benedictine rule.

The monks were admonished to be more strict in their application of the rules of hospitality, and in particular to confine their reception of females to ladies of high quality, and their retinue.

Inspections continued and in 1283 the Bishop of Chichester employed his disciplinary powers to deprive Prior John de Wynton of his office when he was found guilty of promiscuity.

As a result of the Priory becoming increasingly independent of Lessay it was able to escape the fate of other 'alien' priories when in the reign of Edward II, Boxgrove was included in the prescribed list of alien houses, and it's revenues confiscated by the Crown. However, a petition from the Priory in 1383 stating that its members had been time out of mind natives of this realm and always elected a prior from their own number, secured a restitution from Edward III, and Boxgrove was declared 'denizen'. From that time on, the Prior received the monks' professions.

The Priory also enjoyed a visit from Edmund Rich, Archbishop of Canterbury, on his way into exile at Pontigny because of his dispute with King Henry III over his archiepiscopal revenues. He stopped on his way to France at Boxgrove, and consecrated Howel-ap-Ednevet as bishop of St Asaph. Edmund took with him into exile his Chancellor, Richard of Wyke. After the death of Edmund in 1242 Richard returned to England where he became bishop of Chichester. Both men were canonised soon after death; St Edmund by Pope Innocent IV in 1247, St Richard by Pope Urban IV in 1262.

The visits of these great men must have been exciting for the local people. The Priory provided them not only with news but also entertainment and a vital commercial outlet. In 1235 Henry III granted to Boxgrove a licence to hold an annual fair to coincide with its patronal festival of St Blaise which takes place on February the third. The right to hold a fair was always highly prized as these fairs presented an opportunity to buy and sell everything which people needed in those times, including wool. Fairs brought people into the area who in turn brought their custom and in doing so increased the prosperity of the community.

St Blaise together with the Virgin Mary are the patron saints of the Priory. St Blaise was an early fourth century martyr, bishop of Sebaste in Cappadocia, and was the patron saint of woolcombers, probably because before execution he had been tortured by having his body scraped with wool combs (see XI in colour section). The Monks, as Benedictines, were encouraged to work on outdoor pursuits and were enthusiastic sheep farmers. Consequently, they became actively involved in the wool trade, probably selling their wool at the annual fair which took place on either side of the date of their patronal festival. Today we still honour the saint on February the third, in a service during which the throats of the congregation are blessed. This is because St Blaise was said to have removed a fish bone from a small child's throat and thus was thought to have healing powers over diseases of the throat, or maybe, as a visiting priest once suggested, it was because he was executed by having his throat cut.

The monks of Boxgrove were not always the saintly figures which one would expect from followers of the Rule of St Benedict. Sometimes they would 'murmur' amongst themselves to such an extent that Simon, Bishop of Chichester, wrote to the Abbot of Lessay complaining that the Boxgrove monks were 'contumacious' and disobedient. 'And some who were contentious and frequently stirred up strife amongst the brethren'.

The Abbot of Lessay reported the matter to the Holy See, to no less a person than Pope Innocent III, who, in 1209, addressed a Bull to the Abbot saying: 'You have informed us that some of your monks in the priory of Boxgrove are disobedient to you - compel them to observe the Rule.'

Not only were the monks argumentative, but there was often friction between them and the Vicar of the parish church as to their respective rights and privileges. In 1409 there was such a dispute between the monks and the vicar. The monks said that the vicar owed fealty to them. The monks claimed 'altar oblations' and other offerings as belonging to them, in particular the pence accruing at the triennial anniversaries, and all other 'mass pence', as they were commonly called, given during the forty days of Lent and at all other times when they were received by the vicar; and that he was bound to account to the monks for them.

They complained that he didn't join the monks in processions, and in the celebration of Vespers on certain solemn festivals.

They also disputed the vicar's 'right' to a tithe of garden herbs (de decimis olerum). The monks considered the vicar's use to be restricted whilst the vicar claimed unlimited use of the garden produce.

The matter was put to the Bishop of Chichester who decided for the monks. 'The Vicar of the church owed fealty to the Prior and Convent of Boxgrove.'

The oblations and offerings were to be restored to the Prior. The Vicar was to walk in procession with the monks. He was to join in Vespers on all festival days and help in the services on those days. A stall was assigned to him in the choir, and a particular place in the processions.

There had been previous disputes between the Vicar and the Prior, over garden herbs and vegetables. In 1250 there is a deed which says that the tithe to which the Vicar is entitled should include onions and coleworts.

Thus the picture we have of the Priory by the end of the fifthteenth century is of a large building, part Norman in style, part Early English, half of which was the parish church, with a separate house for the Prior and his guests and accommodation for passing travellers. The monastic community consisted of a number of fiercely independently minded monks who grumbled about practical matters with the Vicar, yet they continued day and night to sing the services laid down for them by their founder, St Benedict. They also gave daily alms to the needy from the surrounding parishes, ran a school, and provided a hospital. The Vicar, in his parochial part of the building, looked after the spiritual needs of the parishioners of Boxgrove and Halnaker.

At this point it may be interesting to see how the monastic community was organised and take a look at the daily life of the monks.

At the head of the community was the Prior. (The Abbot was the head of the mother house in Lessay.) To him was due all honour and respect as the spiritual head of the Priory and in the words of St Benedict, 'he takes Christ's place'. In the Rule the whole of chapter two is devoted to describing what kind of man the Abbot (Prior in the case of Boxgrove) should be. St Benedict says: 'For he is believed to be the representative of Christ in the monastery, and for that reason is called by a name of his, according to the words of the Apostle: Ye have received the spirit of the adoption of sons, whereby we cry Abba, Father. Therefore the Abbot ought not to teach or ordain or command anything which is against the law of the Lord; on the contrary, his commands and teaching should be infused into the minds of his disciples like the leaven of divine justice.'

All external honour was shown to him. When he passed by, all were expected to stand and bow towards him. In the chapter house and refectory none might sit in their place until he had taken his seat; when he sat in the cloister no-one might take the seat next to him unless he was invited to do so. The Prior's place in the choir was the first stall on the right hand side. During the Office his stall was to be the farthest from the altar, the juniors being in front of him, and placed nearest to the sanctuary steps. At Mass, however, the position was changed; the Prior and seniors being closest to the altar, for the purpose of making the oblations at the Holy Sacrifice, and giving the blessings. If his name was mentioned in any list of duties all bowed on hearing it read out in Chapter, and they did the same when he ordered any prayers to be said or any duty to be performed, even if he wasn't present when the order was published.

Naturally, the whole government of a religious house depended upon the Prior. He was the mainspring of the whole machine, and his permission was required in everything. He appointed all the officials. In the refectory he alone could send for anything, and he was the only one who could admit anyone to the common table. He gave the signal for the Refectorian to ring the signal bell for the meal to start. He could send a special dish to any of the brethren whom he thought needed it, and the brother, when he received it had to bow in acknowledgement.

Whilst every honour was to be given to him, the Rule firmly stated that he must always remember the fact that all this honour was not paid to him personally, but to his office, and to Christ who was regarded and reverenced in him. He must, to quote the Rule, 'Study with paternal solicitude the character, actions, and needs of all the brethren; never forgetting that he will one day have to render to God an account of them all.'

The sub-Prior was mainly concerned with the internal discipline of the community. Appointed by the Prior, his place was next to his superior. He was honoured by all, but some of the more formal observances, such as the brethren rising and bowing when the Prior went past, were omitted in the case of the sub-Prior.

The main officials of a monastery were frequently known by the name of Obedientaries. Various duties were assigned to them, and they possessed extensive powers in their own spheres.

The Cantor or Precentor was one of the most important officials in the monastery. He was both singer, chief librarian and archivist. He should also be a priest of impeccable character. He was responsible for all the services. The names of those who were to take part in the singing of Lessons or Responsories at Matins or other parts of the daily Office were selected by him and no-one could refuse any duty so assigned. What he arranged to be sung had to be sung and what he chose to be read in the refectory had to be read.

The place of the Precentor in the church was always on the right hand of the choir; that of his assistant, the sub-Precentor or Succentor, was on the left. He was the one who was really in charge of the choir, guarding against mistakes in the Divine service. With this end in view he was to select only music that was known to all, and to see that it was sung in the traditional manner. Woe betide any Succentor with innovative ideas!

The Sacrist was in charge of the church fabric and all the sacred plate and vestments as well as the other valuables, reliquaries, and precious ornaments. Thus when the new altar 'frontelles' arrived, blue to match the vestments, from Katherine Wingfield at Halnaker House, it would have been the Sacrist who received them and put them to use.

The Sacrist was also responsible for cleanliness in the church. Every Saturday he had to see that the sconces of the candlesticks were all scoured out, and that the pavements in front of the altars were washed and cleaned. He had to see to the change of the linen cloths on the altar and the making of the altar breads. He and his assistants were always to be dressed in clean white albs, and when they were cleaning the altar vessels, psalms and other prayers were said.

The Sacrist had to care for the cemetery where the dead brethren were laid to rest. He was to keep it neat and tidy, with the grass cut and trimmed, and the walks free from weeds. No animals were allowed to feed amongst the graves or to disturb the peace of 'God's acre'.

The Sacrist also had the care of the bells, especially those which summoned the brethren to the church; and of the clock, where there was one, and this clock could be touched only by himself or one of his assistants. He had to take care of the lighting of the whole Priory, and see to the provision of candles. From his store he had to supply the church with all necessary lights for the altars, for the choir, and for illuminating the candelabras on feast days. He also had to see to the lighting of the cloister and the dormitories, so that the brethren could see their way down to the church for night services.

The Cellarer had to buy all the food for the community. In this capacity he had to supervise the corn coming in from the granges, and the flour from the mill, and see what was needed of meat, fish, vegetables and beer. The mill may have been the windmill on Halnaker hill which was noted as present in 1301 in the will of Robert de St John. The Cellarer was the 'Martha' of the establishment, often away buying supplies, exempt for much of the time from regular choir duty. He was always much respected because meal times would have been very important to the brethren, tired and cold from their work in the fields or in the cloisters, and from the chanting of the Office in the choir. Under a lax Cellarer the morale of the community would be at a low ebb.

The Refectorian had charge of the Refectory and was responsible for the meals that were provided for the brethren. He would have worked closely with the Cellarer. The Refectorian had to see that there were enough benches and tables and that they were in good repair. He also had to buy cloths and napkins, jugs, dishes and anything else the monks might require. Five times a year he had to renew the rushes that were strewn about the hall, and on Holy Saturday, by custom, he was supposed to scatter bay leaves to scent the air and to give a festal spring-like appearance to the Priory. In summer he might spread flowers about, with mint and fennel, to purify the air.

Amongst the Refectorian's other duties was his care of the lavatory. He was to provide water, hot if necessary, for washing purposes, and was always to provide a clean towel for general use. All towels of any kind were to be changed twice a week, on Sundays and Thursdays.

The Kitchener's responsibilities were formidable. He had to be a man of equable disposition, and, 'always ready to return a mild answer to those who came to him.'

The Kitchener had under him a trust-worthy servant, called the 'Emptor' or buyer. He was responsible for looking after the store-house and seeing that the Kitchener had sufficient provisions to satisfy the needs of the Community. Sometimes the Kitchener received special revenues, provided by the Prior, to meet the expenses of his own table. Often a proportion of the rents of properties owned by the Priory were put aside for this purpose. Often the Community received payments in kind - such as 'some sticks of eels', or a side of venison. Always the Kitchener had to check the provisions as they arrived, see that the eggs were fresh, the meat sound and the fish in good condition.

He had to see that the larder was kept clean, that there were always fresh rushes to put down on the refectory floor, and that the fish was covered with damp reeds to keep it fresh. He had to be careful about his keys. They were always kept in his room and no-one was to touch them without his permission. He was to keep a watchful eye on all the cooks and servants who worked for him. Amongst the many things the Kitchener had to provide for the community was some of the best beer to give to the Precentor and, when required, pigments to mix ink for the writers.

The Kitchener, of course, would have had servers to help him at meal-times, and would have supervised them to see that meals were served promptly and discreetly. Servers were changed quite frquently, usually on Sundays after Lauds, and received a blessing before they took over their duties. They were responsible for drawing water to wash with, and on Saturdays they had to prepare hot and cold water, with towels, in the cloister, for the weekly feet-washing. They had to see that the lavatory was clean, and that all the vessels they used were returned and accounted for by Saturday night.

The Infirmarian looked after the sick members of the Community, and the old and infirm monks. If there was a hospital, as there was at Boxgrove, he looked after everyone who came there. He also had to provide medicines for his patients, and see that they received regular meals from the refectory. He always slept in the infirmary as he had to be ready for any emergency. Most of the treatment for the sick relied on herbs, and the Infirmarian always had to see that there were plenty of these, either dried or fresh, in his store cupboards. He had always to keep a good supply of ginger, cinnamon, peony, etc., so that he could minister some soothing cordial when necessary.

Sometimes the Infirmarian recommended blood-letting as a routine preventative measure against disease. At that time it was believed that fevers, apoplexy and headache followed from an excessive build up of blood and that regular bleeding would keep the monks healthy. The operation was performed four times a year, if possible in February, April, September and October. It was not to take place in the time of harvest, in Advent or Lent, or on the three days following the feasts of Christmas, Easter or Pentecost. The Community attended in groups, from two to six at a time, and a special day would be announced at the proper time that 'those that sat at that table were to be blooded.'

From first to last the operation of blood-letting occupied four days. When the time came the Infirmarian lit a fire in the room set aside for this purpose, and there the operator set to work on his victims. If they wished, the monks who were going to be bled could go to the refectory and take something to eat and drink. Afterwards, when the wound was healing, the monks were allowed special concessions. The daily routine was relaxed until the patient felt fit enough to return to his duties. He was never to bend down to do penance of any kind, for fear of displacing the bandages, and he was to go out of church before the others for fear of having his arm rubbed if he were to walk in file. In the refectory a monk who had been 'blooded' received the same food as the rest with the addition of half a pound of white bread and an extra portion, if possible, of eggs. A dish of soft eggs, sprinkled with salt and parsley and sometimes sage, was usually offered to the patient immediately after the operation.

The Almoner was not necessarily a priest, and his duty was to distribute the alms of the Community to the poor. He had to be of a kind and compassionate disposition, and go to visit the aged poor and the blind and the bedridden outside the monastery. He was never to get impatient with the poor, nor to get angry with them, 'remembering always that they are made in the image of God and redeemed by the blood of Christ.'

The Almoner also superintended the daily maundy, or washing the feet of the poor selected for that purpose. After the morning Mass the Almoner went to the door of the Priory and from the number waiting for alms he chose three, who subsequently had their feet washed by the Prior. Then they were fed and sent away with a small present of money. On the great maundy, that is the Thursday before Easter, it was the Almoner's duty to select the twelve poor whose feet were to be washed and after that they had their meal and received a penny given to them by the monk who had washed their feet.

The Almoner was also in charge of the school. At Boxgrove there was such a school and we know that at the time of the Dissolution there were six boys there. He was also in charge of the mortuary rolls and saw to it that relatives were informed following a death.

Other important functionaries in a Community such as Boxgrove were the Guest-master, who was to see to the comfort of any guests, and the Chamberlain, who looked after the clothes of the monks. It is interesting to note that, at Boxgrove, the monk's clothes were paid for out of the tithe collected from the village of North Mundham. The Chamberlain also made sure that when the monks clothes needed repairing, that was done promptly. He was responsible for the arrangements for shaving the monks. One of the brothers would be appointed as barber. When the time came for a general 'rasura', (shaving the head to produce a tonsure), the Community would sit silently in two lines, one along the cloister wall and the other facing them with their backs to the windows. The general shaving was made a religious act by the recitation of psalms. Usually the monks tonsures were shaved every three weeks, but there was always a special shaving on the eve of the great festivals.

The Master of the Novices was one of the most important functionaries, because, for the year of his probation the novice was in complete subjection to this master. From then on until he made his full profession as a monk, every detail of his behaviour was observed, and corrected, if necessary. The cloister was the novices' schoolroom, and usually the eastern side was assigned to them. At the end of the year, if the Community accepted the new monk, a ceremony marked his passage from the world into the new religious life. His hood was fastened over his face three days before the ceremony of acceptance. Then, just as Christ was buried in the tomb for three days to rise again, so, after Mass on the third day after the monk's hood was closed, the Prior unfastened the hood and the late novice joined the ranks of the junior monks who still remained under the eye and guidance of the Junior Master.

Lastly there would be the Hebdomadarian, the priest appointed for the week to lead all the Offices. He also gave all the blessings that might be required, for instance on the holy water, the candles and the ashes for special days.

In the case of a small community such as Boxgrove Priory, many of these officials would undertake double duties, and some would be omitted altogether, but we can be sure that, under the Benedictine Rule, the daily life of the monks

DAILY LIFE IN A MONASTERY

The times are approximate and would vary between monasteries

MATINS -	Midnight. They descended to the church by the night stair led by one of their number.
LAUDS -	followed straight on after Matins. About 1.30 am. they returned to bed.
PRIME -	6.00 am.
TERCE -	8.00am.
BREAKFAST	
CHAPTER MEETING. The daily assembly.	
HIGH MASS -	10.30 am.
DINNER -	11.30 am.
NONE -	12.30 pm.
RELAXATION	work in the fields or garden or manuscript copying
VESPERS -	5.00 pm.
SUPPER	
COMPLINE -	7.00 pm.
BED -	7.30 pm in winter; 8.30 in summer.

would have proceeded in a strict and seemly fashion.

The lives of the monks revolved around the daily services, known collectively as the Opus Dei.

The day started with Matins which took place usually at midnight, or sometimes a bit later. The Sacrist would ring a small bell, the monks would rise, cross themselves, and put on their night boots. The Calling Bell began to toll, and they would go down the night stair and take their places in the choir, the junior monks nearest the altar. Although the dormitory has gone, traces of the night stair leading from it to the choir can still be seen in the north transept of the Priory. The Prior was the last to arrive. He would signal the bell to stop. Everyone rose, returned the Prior's greeting and bowed down for triple prayer, Pater, Ave, Creed. The night Office always began with these prayers.

Matins was followed almost immediately by Lauds, usually around one o'clock in the morning. Then the monks went back to bed.

Between six and seven o'clock they would return to the church for Prime followed by Terce. Then they would take a light breakfast called the Mixtum. Usually this consisted of a quarter of a pound of bread and a third of a pint of wine or beer. This was eaten in silence and standing. In Lent, the Mixtum was not taken except on Sundays.

The Chapter meeting took place around nine o'clock in the morning. It started with a sacred reading, then the novices left. The rest discussed any matter that needed discussion, and anyone who confessed to some infringement of the Rule would be corrected.

After the final Commemoration of the departed the Chapter was concluded with the De Profundis.

Before High Mass, at about half past ten, the monks would go to the cloister, when, at the triple sounding of the tabula, a piece of wood to which two other pieces of wood were loosely fastened, the signal was given for seemly conversation. One particular part of the cloister was selected for these conversations, which were known as 'Parliaments'. The juniors went to the western part of the cloister, others to the northern walk, where the seniors could be consulted. Conversation was to be concerned only with spiritual issues.

At half past ten all went to church for High Mass. The senior members now took their seats nearest to the altar. There were many processions in those days during the services, and much sprinkling of holy water. On Wednesdays and Fridays in Lent the community would walk barefoot around the cloister as a penitential exercise. The Prior always celebrated at the high altar on great feast days, always with full ceremony. Four times a year there would be exceptionally solemn processions with relics and banners.

Dinner followed High Mass, preceded by a washing of hands. This would be about half past eleven. The meal consisted of bread, soup, vegetables, sometimes meat, more often fish. Usually there was beer to drink but sometimes wine. The directions for the serving of this meal are very elaborate, but politeness was always emphasised and the importance of looking after other diner's needs before one's own. After the meal the leftovers would be collected up and given by the almoner to the poor.

The service after dinner was called None, and then everyone could go out to work in the garden or in the fields; some monks might work at copying or illuminating manuscripts and the juniors could relax with games and exercise. St Benedict realised the importance of relaxation for the monks. Without relaxation, he said, 'as bows always bent', they would lose the power of 'aiming straight at perfection'. Monks should not be gloomy people.

In summer the Community would often have an hour's sleep, or at least take some sort of rest during the afternoon.

Vespers would take place at five o'clock in the winter and six in the summer. This would be followed by supper, a light meal, then back to church for Compline. Then, at seven in winter, and eight in summer, the monks would go to the dormitory to sleep until the Sacrist woke them for Matins.

Thus the monks of Boxgrove would have spent orderly days, the mornings being passed in prayer and conducting the chief business of the Community; the afternoons devoted to work, both manual and intellectual, and to recreation. They were expected to work in the fields, and those who were best suited copied manuscripts and illuminated the margins. In all, it was a very satisfying life for those who had the vocation, and although it seems hard that they had to get up at night for the night services, they still had about eight hours sleep in all because they went to bed early.

Maybe, as time passed, some of the monastic houses didn't always live up to the high standards laid down in the Rule. Boxgrove, one of the smaller monastic houses, did become a trifle lax on occasions, and had to be admonished by the Bishop of Chichester after an inspection.

There are a set of injunctions given to the Prior and Convent of Boxgrove in 1518 by the Bishop after an inspection. In these he noted how the numbers of the monks were declining and ordered that more were to be admitted.

He reminded them that the tolling of the bell for Prime should take place at the due hour and that the elders as well as the younger members of the Community should walk to the service in pairs, both when going and returning. Perhaps the monks were tempted to rush back to bed when the service was over.

It was recommended that the monks 'should have their countenances, as they walk, cast down to earth, or reverently raised to a crucifix and that they should sing at the same time lowly, devoutly and methodically, blessing God with one voice.'

They were also reminded that the novices should keep their habits clean, and that the dormitories should be kept cleaner. Everyone was to eat at the same time, listen to sacred lessons, sleep at the same time and rise at the same time. They must keep silence when appropriate.

They should never be unemployed 'lest the Devil should find them idle.' The monks were never to wander outside the enclosure of the Priory without permission. They were to be content with their diet and abstain from drinking or feasting together, 'or other gluttonies'. Neither should they indulge in 'vain talkings together.'

In general, the Bishop's inspectors urged a stronger observance of the Rule. Apparently some of the monks had taken to wearing fancy shoes, 'tied with many laces.' It was known that the Prior liked archery competitions and he was told to keep such activities within the enclosure of the Priory. There were to be no games of dice or cards and no drinking or gossiping (confabulationes) taking place in the churchyard or cemetery.

Finally, the monks were to be wary of women. The Injunctions stipulate that 'certain offices, which are usually done more by women than men, such as to wash linen suitably, to milk cows, to churn butter, and to make cheeses,' should be done by persons suitable, and things taken to them should be carried by a man 'free from suspicion' and brought back by the same man, ' in order to remove any sinister opinion which may by such occasions, occur in such matters.'

For four hundred years there were monks at Boxgrove. They would have been a familiar sight to everyone living in the area. The Almoner would have been seen visiting the sick and the buyer of provisions going about his tasks. The villagers would have noticed the comings and goings of visitors to the Priory, some of them, like St Edmund Rich, very important people indeed. They would have heard the bell tolling the times of services, they would have seen the monks working in the fields and tending their stock. The poor and the sick in the villages would have gone to the Priory to receive alms. The boys would have attended the school. Some of the men would have been admitted to the Community as novices and then as fully professed monks.

Then, in the reign of Henry VIII, all this would be swept aside by parliamentary legislation, and Boxgrove Priory lost it's monks, and changed it's direction for the next four hundred years.

THE SEAL OF BOXGROVE PRIORY

There is, in the British Museum, the matrix, or mould, for the seal of the Priory of Boxgrove, still in such good condition that excellent impressions can be struck. There were almost certainly other seals made for the Priory at different times, the one in the Museum being from the late thirteenth century.

Seals were used as the signature marks for people or communities. A unique design engraved or cast in a hard material was impressed on heat softened wax

Figure 20. The Seal of Boxgrove Priory dating from the late 13th century

which, when hard, could then be attached to a document as carrying the authority of the owner of the seal. Many seals were lost at the time of the Dissolution of the Monasteries but a number have been found by chance. In the catalogue of British seal-dies in the British Museum, there is a record of a Boxgrove seal found with another seal in a vessel dug up in Bonner's Fields, Hackney, London. We also know that some labourers at work in excavating a railway line, dug up an earthen pot or urn, in which were found two original brass moulds. The most important of these seals proved to be a seal of Boxgrove Priory.

The obverse represents the west front of a church building, probably a stylised view of the Priory church. In its upper part within a trefoil is a quarter-length figure of God the Father, his hand raised in blessing. Below him can just be seen the Holy Spirit in the form of a dove descending towards the full-length figures of the Archangel Gabriel and the Blessed Virgin Mary. The whole composition thus represents the Annunciation within an architectural framework. On either side of this group are two small figures of kneeling monks, doubtless representing the Boxgrove community. Below is the head of a Bishop, representing St Blaise, co-patron with the Virgin of the Priory.

Around the edge of this side of the seal runs the inscription:

Sigillum ecclesie Sancte Marie
Sanctique Blasii de Boxgrava.
(The seal of the church of St Mary
and St Blaise of Boxgrove).

The reverse shows the Blessed Virgin Mary seated under a canopy, with the infant Jesus on her lap. He raises his hand in blessing, she holds a lily sceptre. On either side are trees with birds in them. The Virgin's feet rest on an elegant corbel. Round the margin appears the following rhyming inscription with the obvious (but wrong) derivation of the name of Boxgrove from a grove of box trees:

Dicitur ex ligno
viridi Boxgravia digno,
nomine nam crescit,
virtutibus atque virescit.

(Boxgrove is appropriately named after the green tree for it grows and flourishes with virtues).

THE DISSOLUTION OF THE PRIORY

In the early years of the reign of Henry VIII (See XII in colour section) both the Halnaker House estate and Boxgrove Priory appeared to be entering an era of increased influence and prosperity. Lord De La Warr clearly had ambitions to rival the great family of the Montagues at Midhurst and, as well as embellishing the Priory church, he began a major program of improvement and extension to Halnaker House itself. Architectural historians consider that when his works were completed his seat had been transformed into one of the finest Tudor style houses ever built and fit to receive Edward VI as a guest for several days in 1552.

In addition to these works the Priory was in train to restore its reputation as a religious institution. This was the result of reforms by a new Prior, Thomas Myles, elected in 1524, and operating under the vigilant eye of Bishop Sherborne, an immediate neighbour in his official residence of Aldingbourne House.

It is obvious, however, that neither Lord De La Warr nor the Bishop had in any way anticipated the major policy changes to be initiated by Henry VIII in the 1530s, nor the effect that these would have on their relatively isolated community.

Cardinal Wolsey took advantage of a meeting of the abbots and priors of Benedictine houses held on 12 November 1521 to stress the necessity and urgency of reform (See XIV in colour section). By a papal bull granted in 1524 he obtained full and sole powers to visit and reform the 'exempt' orders, into which category fell, of course, nearly all monasteries, nunneries and friaries. There were many small establishments surviving with a minimal number of members, but still possessed of sizeable properties and some revenues. He took advantage of the situation to dissolve twenty nine religious houses in the five year period 1524-1529, and divert the revenues and assets of the greater number of them to the new college he himself had founded at Oxford, known today as Magdalen. He was aided in this programme by the fact that in November 1528 he obtained a further papal bull specifically authorising the suppression of any monastery with less than six inmates, and granting powers to enforce the merger of any house with less than twelve into a larger institution.

Wolsey's principal agent in this programme was Thomas Cromwell (See XV in colour section), who, when he rose to power in his turn, undoubtedly saw the opportunities for the enrichment of the Crown that an extended and more ruthless application of these powers could afford. The break with the Roman Church provided the opportunity to put his project into effect.

However, before any policy could be adopted by the King it was, of course, necessary to establish the actual level of ecclesiastical assets, liabilities and incomes, and Cromwell was able to take advantage of proposals to modify the basis of church taxation, which were already in hand before the break with Rome, to establish and verify the value of all ecclesiastical benefices. Commissioners were appointed for each county in January 1535, and they reported with such commendable speed that by the beginning of 1536 all their reports were in the hands of the Exchequer. The resultant digest of these reports was called the Valor Ecclesiasticus, and is an invaluable source of information even today.

The report on Boxgrove Priory stated that at that date there were nine monks and novices, eight labourers, twelve servants, six pensioners and eight children, a total of 43 souls. The report did not state whether the children were choir boys or orphans. The Priory's annual income was declared to be :-

Gross general income (spiritual and temporal)	£186.03.00

The reports forming part of the Valor Ecclesiasticus did not attempt in any way to pass judgment upon the spiritual or material condition of each establishment. To provide justification for the suppression of the religious houses Thomas Cromwell had need of further evidence of their state of decline, and in July 1535 he appointed a small group of special commissioners to visit every establishment.

The reports of these commissioners (compiled into a volume called Comperta) presented in general a deplorable picture of declining standards, immorality and corruption in the monasteries and was undoubtedly influential in obtaining rapid consent to the Act of Suppression which was presented for approval by Parliament in March 1536. The report was largely accepted as factual at the time, and subsequent generations of historians have accepted it as evidence that the suppression of the monasteries was fully justified.

The Act of Suppression gave permission, at the sovereign's discretion, for the suppression of the smaller religious communities: the preamble referred to the corruption prevailing in communities less than a dozen strong: 'For as much as manifest sin, vicious, carnal and abominable living is daily used and committed amongst the little and small abbeys, priories and other religious houses of monks, canons and nuns, where the congregation of such religious persons is under the number of 12 persons....': but it is significant that the actual definition of a small establishment enshrined in the main text was one possessing a net income of less than £200 per annum.

Assent to the Act having been speedily obtained, instructions were sent on the 24th April 1536 to each county to form a commission to report on the general state of each religious house, its financial situation, including a fresh assessment of its annual revenues, and whether the inmates wished to transfer to a larger establishment unaffected by the Act or accept a pension in exchange for being released from their vows. These commissioners were essentially composed of local gentry, and it will be noted that their brief was wider in scope than that of their predecessors who had provided the information for the Valor Ecclesiasticus.

A recent generation of historians has examined the reports of these commissioners, and in many cases have discovered striking discrepancies between their reports and those of Cromwell's special commissioners which formed the basis of the Comperta. The general conclusion of writers of all schools of history has been that a small group of unscrupulous and personally ambitious men fully understood the true purpose behind Cromwell's instructions and took good care to produce the type of evidence which he required for public consumption.

Boxgrove Priory was, of course, a prime candidate for suppression, and it was particularly unfortunate that its visitation was conducted by Richard Layton, described as being the most energetic and resourceful of Cromwell's commissioners but possessing a complete lack of principle. His visitation of Boxgrove must have been quite rushed, as his reports indicate that on 1st October 1536 he rode from Hampshire to Lewes whilst visiting Boxgrove en route - a considerable feat considering the state of the highways in that age. He saw fit to report that the Prior of Boxgrove had two mistresses, and that his monks were of the same pattern. The fact that a Bishop's visitation of 1527 and the subsequent report of the dissolution commissioners mentioned no cases of promiscuity amongst the monks of Boxgrove is often cited as a justification for the doubts expressed by modern historians as to the accuracy of the Comperta.

Many courtiers and local nobility saw great possibilities for personal enrichment in the situation created by the Act of Suppression and promptly approached either Cromwell or the King in person to solicit receiving the properties of their local religious establishment as a reward for their previous services to the Crown. The letter addressed from Halnaker House by Lord De La Warr in respect of Boxgrove Priory had, however, a significantly different purpose.

In this letter Thomas West referred to his relationship to Boxgrove Priory as that of the founding family, that his ancestors' tombs were all to be found in the monastery church, that he had recently built a burial chapel for himself, and that the parish church was an integral part of the monastery buildings. He accordingly requested that discretion be used to forbear its suppression or alternatively that it be converted into a college for secular canons, failing which he requested that the entire estate be transferred to him.

This first approach was unsuccessful in that the suppression of the Priory was confirmed, and a subsequent petition from Lord De La Warr and Elizabeth, his wife, is recorded in the *Letters and Papers of Henry VIII* requesting that :-

(1) The unspoiled monastic church be retained as the parish church.

(2) They be given permission to buy the ornaments.

(3) The bells be left in place.

(4) The founders lodging be permitted to stand, with all houses of office.

(5) They be given the demesnes to farm.

(6) They be given the rights to the parsonage of Boxgrove and three other parishes with the tithes and certain stated rents to an annual value of £78.00.11 1/2d.

This approach found favour (save he was permitted to retain only three of the five bells), and appropriate instructions were sent immediately to the commissioners of Sussex (Sir John Daintree of Petworth, William Palmer of Angmering and John Morise) who reported to Thomas Cromwell on 26 March 1537 that the Priory had been dissolved and the transaction completed to the satisfaction of Lord De La Warr. The commissioners' report gave full details of the sums raised in respect of livestock, standing crops, furniture and fittings and the bells, and they were able to report that the total proceeds were £276.10.11d. In addition 334 ounces of silver to an estimated value of £65.3.1d had been despatched to the Court of Augmentation in London. Lord De La Warr's contribution to this total was £125.13.4d, of which £40.00.0d was paid immediately with the balance due the following Michaelmas and Easter. The commissioners took care to point out that this was the most profitable disposal of ecclesiastical property in West Sussex at that time for the benefit of the Crown.

Upon the dissolution of the Priory eight of the nine inmates applied for licences (called capacities), entitling them to seek employment as parish priests elsewhere. They received between them the sum of £33.13.0d as King's Alms and payments on account of pensions, with permission to take with them their individual beds. It is recorded that Thomas Myles, the last Prior, eventually became Rector of New Shoreham in 1548, whilst another monk, Sir Thomas Masson, succeeded in becoming Rector of East Bletchingley in the same year. There are records of brothers becoming curate or chantry priests in the diocese, one of whom, Richard Hedde, was still drawing his pension of £5.00.0d per annum in 1558 whilst also serving as a curate at Bepton.

It will be seen that the happy accident that the head of the founding family was both a personage of local social importance and a member of the King's Council gave every incentive to Thomas Cromwell to accede to an arrangement which would provoke no local dissent. This was all the more true as Lord De La Warr is recorded as having taken the necessary steps to preserve the assets of the Priory before its actual dissolution, so that Cromwell was also able to demonstrate that the transaction was of considerable financial benefit to the Crown. For his part Lord De La Warr was able to preserve the architectural heritage of the Boxgrove Priory buildings, retain his local influence by acquiring the direct right to the patronage of the parish and combine the two local major estates into one entity.

A combination of many long standing local economic grievances and popular resentment of the suppression of the monasteries, known in many rural areas as kindly landlords and the only source of local charity, led to much resistance to Henry's policies. In the autumn of 1536 there were, indeed, a number of serious rebellions in the North of England, collectively called the Pilgrimage of Grace.

Henry was able to overcome these local revolts by a combination of improvised forces and duplicitous negotiations whilst substantially maintaining his policies unchanged. But his reaction to the depth of feeling against these as revealed at the time, led him to adopt an attitude to all public expression of dissent which must be described as both autocratic and, indeed, paranoid, and which set in train a series of events which would materially affect the future of Boxgrove Priory.

The Act of Supremacy of 1534 which had confirmed Henry as Supreme Head of the English Church had been accompanied by the Treason Act. This imposed the penalty for treason on all who maliciously spoke, wrote or acted in such a way as to deprive the King of any dignity, title or name of his royal estate. In the period immediately following the suppression of the Pilgrimage of Grace this Act was employed in all its severity.

The terms of the Treason Act, in fact, implied that any previous statement of dissent was a criminal act, absolution for which could not be obtained by swearing a new oath of allegiance as had often been the practice in the past. When one takes into account that in that age there were no strict rules as to the admissibility of hearsay evidence, nor any restrictions as to the period during which a suspect might be held in detention for the purposes of interrogation, and that the normal punishment for treason had always been execution, the severity of this new measure can be fully appreciated. Henry and Cromwell pursued suspected opponents of their policies with the utmost vigour, with a resultant reign of terror throughout England. An outside observer, the French Ambassador, could only comment 'I think few lords in this country are safe', and there is ample evidence that many persons of more humble status forfeited their lives.

Lord De La Warr was particularly unfortunate in that both of the leading families in Sussex, with whom he was known to be on intimate terms, were part of the extended royal family. The Marquis of Exeter, whose seat was on the Sussex/Hampshire border was in fact the heir to the throne, as grandson of Edward IV in the Yorkist line, as long as Henry had no lawful heirs. In this dynastic age Exeter was obviously regarded by the King with great suspicion as a possible usurper, and had already once been committed to the Tower in 1531 on suspicion that he was plotting to raise an assembly of supporters.

The other leading family in the county was that of the Countess of Salisbury and her children, namely Lord Montague and Geoffrey and Reginald Pole, who also figured, if more distantly, in the royal line of succession.

All of these nobles were conservative in their religious beliefs, and the Montague family came, at a later date, to be recognised as the leading Catholic recusants in the area. Inculcated in their pride of status they did not hesitate to declare in public that they looked forward to a more congenial regime when Henry was no longer on the throne. Reginald had gone so far as to choose the path of exile and the biretta of a Cardinal of the Holy Roman faith. Henry regarded him as guilty of high treason and an active plotter against his regime and for some years now had kept a close watch on his movements on the Continent through various government agents. On the domestic front there was no lack of venal informers to lay information as to the sayings and doings of these nobles in Sussex, whom the monarch regarded as a cohesive group.

The first information implicating them in serious dissent emanated from the Earl of Southampton, Henry's Lord Admiral, who reported on September 1538 that various witnesses had second hand evidence to the effect that Sir Geoffrey Pole intended to raise a body of men and flee abroad with them to support and protect his brother, the Cardinal, who he learned might be assassinated by Henry's agents. Almost simultaneously Sir Geoffrey's servant, Hugh Holland, was arrested and transported to London for interrogation, on suspicion of having carried correspondence from the family to the Cardinal in exile.

By early October Sir Geoffrey had, himself, been interred in the Tower of London, where he unsuccessfully attempted to commit suicide before he could be interrogated. He was subsequently submitted to a series of brutal, consecutive interrogations, which were successful in the sense that he made statements implicating a wide circle of his acquaintances in Sussex. In particular he testified that he and others 'would wish a change in the world, without meaning any hurt to the King', and on being pressed to name these others he cited the names of Lord De La Warr, George Croftes (Chancellor of Chichester Cathedral) and the Marquis of Exeter, even whilst stating that he had not spoken to the latter for over two years.

Various others witnesses testified that both Lord Montague and Sir Geoffrey had burned correspondence in their respective houses, whilst a priest, Sir Henry Owen, bore witness in November that Lord De La Warr had said 'a time will come that God will punish for the plucking down of abbeys' and that he knew him to be very intimate with the Marquis of Exeter, whilst George Croftes in his interrogation testified that Lord De La Warr had never changed his opinion 'touching praying to saints, pilgrimages, free will and justification'.

It was on slight evidence such as this that Henry required a commission of his Council to report as to whether Lord De La Warr had committed acts which would justify him being committed to the Tower. To Henry's obvious displeasure this commission reported on 1 December 1538 that they could 'find as yet no sufficient ground to commit him to the Tower'.

In this atmosphere it is not surprising that Lord De La Warr, then aged 66, was seized with panic. It is known that he consulted Richard Sampson, Bishop of Chichester, as to his best course of action, but received little comfort save for a general exhortation that he would come to no harm if he spoke the truth. This guidance must be judged in the context of subsequent knowledge that Sampson himself felt in disfavour for displaying too little support for the reformation programme. It is typical of the zeal with which such investigations were pursued, and the general climate of suspicion that Sampson was called to testify to the King's Council of the details of this harmless conversation.

The reign of terror continued, and two days later, on 3 December 1538, Lord De La Warr was committed, notwithstanding, to the Tower for interrogation, no formal charge having been brought at this time. Lord Montague and the Marquis of Exeter were less fortunate as on the same day they were confined to the Tower on charges of High Treason, from which few escaped alive. They were indeed beheaded quite promptly on Tower Hill on 8 December 1538, whilst on the same day Dr Croftes and Hugh Holland were found guilty and hung, drawn and quartered at Tyburn.

Lord De La Warr was certainly fortunate in that of all suspected members of the so-called Exeter Conspiracy he alone escaped with his life. This has been attributed to the scanty evidence against him, and perhaps more importantly to the fact that as a baron he was entitled to be judged by his peers and Henry could not be certain of obtaining the desired verdict. It is typical of the atmosphere of the time that even whilst Lord De La Warr was confined in the Tower informants in quest of personal gain were still submitting malicious evidence, an example of which may be found in the *Letters and Papers of Henry VIII* - 'At my Lord's place in Halnaker there is coming by night and riding also by night to and fro.... My Lord should be examined and his house searched, for surely this riding to and fro is to put evidence out of the way.'

After eighteen days of confinement Henry and Cromwell were obliged, nevertheless, to discharge Lord De La Warr from the Tower on 21 December 1538, on his providing a recognisance in the sum of three thousand pounds 'for his personal appearance before the King and Council, when called on, within a year's date'.

Henry's apparent intention was to demolish the local political base of the supposed participants in the Exeter Conspiracy, and in due course he achieved this purpose in a variety of ways. The Countess of Salisbury was confined to the Tower for several years, and was eventually executed in 1541 despite the fact that no new incriminating evidence had been discovered.

Within a year of his discharge from the Tower, Lord De La Warr was placed under pressure to exchange his estate of Halnaker for the Benedictine nunnery of Wherwell, near Andover. A letter dated 8 November 1539 is recorded from Lady Elizabeth to Thomas Cromwell requesting that this transfer be delayed until after the 1540 harvest. One must assume that this request was successful as it is known that the newly enlarged Halnaker estate became the property of the Crown only in the latter year.

In the meantime the village would have suffered from the disappearance of the Priory as there is no mention in the records of any provision having been made for the children, pensioners and domestic staff who had benefited from its bounty. The estate was now managed by an agent appointed by the Crown, but Halnaker House stood empty with again resultant loss of employment and of the benevolent protection that an influential family could confer on its local community.

The pulpitum screen separating the parish church from the monastic nave was converted into an exterior wall and the villagers transferred their place of worship to the highly decorated Priory church. There would certainly have been little change in the form of service while Sir Thomas Boxfield continued as vicar until 1548, as diocesan records show that successive bishops fell into disfavour for their lack of zeal in implementing the reforms desired by Thomas Cromwell. Thus the parish church continued as a centre of life in Boxgrove for, in an age when attendance at Sunday Mass was considered an obligation, it provided an opportunity for the whole parish to meet at what was as much a social as a religious occasion.

THE KING VISITS HALNAKER

In 1547 Henry VIII died and his son aged nine succeeded to the throne as Edward VI. (See XIII in colour section). In 1552 aged fourteen he and his Court made a progress leaving Greenwich on 27 June for Sussex and Hampshire where they would stay at Petworth, Cowdray and Halnaker. At that time it was common for the Court to visit large estates within reach of the capital so that the heavy cost of maintaining the court could be spread amongst the owners of the great houses visited who were required to provide hospitality.

These progresses took place during the summer months when the drier roads would have been passable to wheeled carriages and the King would have been accompanied by a very considerable company. With him went the Privy Council who were the real governing body of the kingdom at that time, so in addition to his own personal servants and guards, there were armed contingents attached to the principal nobility who made up the Court. J.G. Nicholls, writing in the Sussex Archaeological Collections, describes how, while staying at Petworth it was found necessary to send home many of these followers save 150 picked men. We know this from Edward's journal for he wrote '...the traine was thought to be nier 4000 horse which ware inough to eat up the country; for there was little medow nor hay al the way as I went.'

From Petworth the Court moved to Cowdray. In a letter to a friend Edward describes how 'we have been occupied in killing wild bestes, in pleasant journeys, in good fare in viewing fair countries... and so to Cowdray, a goodly house of Sir Anthony Browne's where we were marvelously, yea, rather excessively banketted.' (See XV1 in colour section). From Cowdray, the Court progressed to reach Halnaker on 27 July 1552. The King described it as 'Halvenaker, a pretty house beside Chichester' which was the seat of Thomas, Lord De La Warr.

The house would have been only large enough to accommodate a small proportion of Edward's numerous traine most of whom were probably lodged in Chichester. We know little of the few days the King spent at Halnaker except that the Privy Council sat there on 30, 31 July and 1 and 3 August.

Edward was becoming increasingly frail and sickly and his courtiers did all that they could to protect him from infections. Should he die the succession would pass to his elder half sister Mary, a fanatical Catholic, with serious implications for the Protestant cause. The plague had been endemic in Europe since 1347 when perhaps a quarter of the population had died from the Black Death. For the following three centuries the plague flared sporadically in cities, spread by rats amongst a crowded populace where the streets were often open sewers, there was no provision for the disposal of garbage and water supplies were infected. Those concerned with Edward's health did what they could to protect him from disease and a proclamation was issued on 8 August as the progress moved into Hampshire: '...for avodying sutch as have taken up theire lodging at Southampton without th'ordr of th'arbergers, with a commandment that other hereafter doe not attempt the like either theare or any other place upon paine of the Kings greate indignation'. And later, 'A proclamation to avoyde all manner of persones infected with pestilence or other contagious diseases or having any person in their houses therewithall infected from the Courte and other places whereunto the Kinges Magestie shall repaire in this his Magesties progresse. And also forbydding any th'inhabitants of Poole or Wynborne Mynster by reason of the plage theare to resort to the Courte at Woodland or Canford during his Magesties abode theare'. Though he escaped the plague, however, the unfortunate Edward died of consumption the following year at Greenwich aged only 16.

Figure 21. A medieval illustration showing a garderobe projecting from the wall of a house, with a cess-pit below. The unfortunate person in the cess-pit has fallen through a broken floorboard. From a 15th century French translation of Boccaccio's Decameron.

HALNAKER MILL

No history of Boxgrove parish would be complete without some account of Halnaker Mill (See IV in colour section). Set 420 feet high on an outlier of the South Downs with uninterrupted winds from all four quarters, it remains a major landmark even if no longer in use. The present construction is described by the experts as a tower-mill with hand wheel winding; indeed, it is claimed as the oldest tower-mill in Sussex, dating from about 1750.

The use of windpower is recorded in Persia as early as the tenth century and it seems likely that windmills would have been seen by Crusaders returning from the East and thus introduced to Western Europe. The earliest record of a windmill in England is that at Lewes, East Sussex in 1155. By 1300 there was certainly one on Halnaker Hill, for when John de St. John died in 1301, the Manor of Halnaker was described as containing 400 acres of arable, 20 acres of meadow, a windmill and a pigeon house. Goodwood Estate records have a lease of 1540 for the manor of 'Halfnaked' detailing the rent of sixteen quarters of corn yearly from 'the farmer of the windmill of said manor'. Other references and maps show that there has been a mill on the site to the present day.

The earliest windmills used cloth sails spread over wooden frames for their sweeps. The whole mill was supported off the ground on a single post and could be rotated by the miller so that the sweeps faced into the wind. A later development was the smock mill, that is, a mill where the main body of the mill does not rotate to face the wind, but only the cap and sweeps. The name 'smock' deriving from the appearance of the whitewashed conical shape of the wooden cladding. A tower-mill is basically a brick-built smock mill; tower-mills were usually tiled or cement-rendered and tarred for protection, with the cap and sweeps remaining white. In operation, the sweeps have to face into the wind. The operation of moving the cap to achieve this is called 'winding', pronounced as in 'win' not as in 'wine'. At Halnaker, this was done by pulling on an endless loop of chain hanging down to ground level at the rear of the cap. In its last years of operation, Halnaker was probably fitted with a small vertically-mounted 'fantail', which turned the cap by the power of the wind until it was itself edge-on to the wind, so bringing the sweeps facing the wind.

The last milling family was that of Watkins, who worked the mill and lived in the mill house close by from 1868 until 1905 when lightning split the mainshaft carrying the sweeps and rendered the mill unusable. No repairs were made and the mill became derelict. In 1934 a major restoration of the outside was carried out by Neves of Heathfield as a memorial to the wife of Sir William Bird, the owner of Eartham House. The damaged wooden wind-shaft was removed and an iron one, specially extended to fit, was put in from Punnett's Town wind saw mill near Heathfield. New sweeps were also fitted. These have since been replaced in 1956 and again in 1994 . The empty brick tower had its windows filled in, and a new sixteen-sided beehive cap put on.

The working mill was four floors high, Halnaker not needing the usual fifth level as there was so much wind available. From the top, the gear floor in the cap, then the bin floor to which the sacks of grain were raised by a hoist, working off the main drive. Below this was the stone floor, where the actual grinding was done, the meal being led off down spouts to the spout floor where it was bagged. Loading was often done from staging above ground level, but there is no evidence for this at Halnaker. It had two pairs of stones, driven from a great spur wheel on the bottom of a vertical shaft, itself being driven by the sweeps on their windshaft with its all- important brake wheel.

Sussex millstones were usually about 4 ft. in diameter weighing about 18 cwt. It is the top or 'runner' stone that moves over the bed stone, the grinding being achieved both by the weight of the stone and the slicing action of the grooves cut in the stones during the 'dressing'. The pattern appears identical when both stones are face-up, so in use with the runner stone face-down, the patterns are opposed and so cut the grain. The stones do not touch, but are adjusted with great accuracy to a hair's breadth apart by the 'tentering gear'.

Generally, a wind of about 10 mph. would start the sweeps; a good working wind is about 20 mph., but even the most modern mills with patent shutters on the sweeps had to apply the brake for safety in winds of 40 mph! The gearing gave a stone rotation of about 100 rpm. It was considered good going to grind two sacks of wheat or one of oats in an hour.

Unlike a water mill, where the miller just lifts his sluice-gates to start work at a time of his choosing, the miller in a windmill was totally dependant on the weather, and might have to remain idle for days or even weeks at a time; or work late into the night, with consequent danger from fire from candles. When he could start, the sweeps needed their sailcloth covers adjusted to suit the conditions. Once they were turning, he could raise the sacks with the hoist and empty them into the bins. He had then to control the rate of flow into the stones and see to the collection of the meal two floors below. All these features needed constant adjustment, so if millers were as plump and jolly as they are depicted in stories, they must have been very fit as well, with good calf muscles from all that ladder climbing!

HA'NACKER MILL

Sally is gone that was so kindly
Sally is gone from Ha'nacker Hill.
And the Briar grows ever since then so blindly
And ever since then the clapper is still,
And the sweeps have fallen from Ha'nacker Mill

Ha'nacker Hill is in Desolation:
Ruin a-top and a field unploughed.
And Spirits that call on a fallen nation
Spirits that loved her calling aloud:
Spirits abroad in a windy cloud.

Spirits that call and no one answers;
Ha'nacker's down and England's done,
Wind and Thistle for pipe and dancers
And never a ploughman under the Sun.
Never a ploughman. Never a one.

Hilaire Belloc

Figure 22. Impression of Hilaire Belloc in 1910. Drawn by David Goodman

Hilaire Belloc who loved Sussex deeply and described its people and countryside colourfully in 'The Four Men', lived for part of his childhood at Slindon around 1880. He would have been there when the windmill at Halnaker was still working and perhaps this left a lasting impression. Later when he lived at Shipley he bought the windmill there and this poem reflects a nostalgia for old times.

THE MORLEYS OF HALNAKER

The disappearance of the monks from the Priory and the De La Warr family from Halnaker House led to significant changes in the pattern of life of the inhabitants of the two hamlets of Halnaker and Boxgrove. Both the De La Warr family and the Priory had been benevolent and conscientious landlords. Both had provided work for the local community. The Priory had not only provided work but also a regular system of poor relief, medical help and a school. The Lords of the Manor of Halnaker had for centuries provided the community with

Figure 23. A study of trees in Halnaker Park by David Goodman.

an effective system of justice. It was going to take nearly fifty years before the community settled down again under a stable system.

Immediately after Lord De La Warr's departure Henry VIII appointed one of the more substantial yeomen of Boxgrove, John Jennyns, as Steward of Boxgrove and Halnaker and Keeper of the House and Park. Over the years the park had been gradually enlarged. In 1440 a licence had been granted to enclose three hundred acres of land and wood within the lordship of Halnaker. In 1552 the park was stated to be four miles around and capable of sustaining eight hundred deer if some provision for hay was made in winter. Today the park contains many fine old trees, notably Spanish (sweet) chestnuts, eighteen of which formed an avenue leading up to the entrance of old Halnaker House. These trees are fast growing and long lived and one in the park was measured recently by Owen Johnson as having a diameter of nearly nine feet about four feet above ground level. Spanish chestnuts were first noted in Sussex in 1768, but an early map of the surroundings of Halnaker House drawn in 1629, shows a row of trees leading up to the entrance (see XVII in colour section). If these are the chestnuts some of which still survive, they may have been planted by John Morley soon after he came to Halnaker. In 1546, the office of Steward of Boxgrove and Halnaker and Keeper of the House and Park, passed to a more important person in the county, Henry, Earl of Arundel. In 1561 Elizabeth 1 granted these holdings to the Earl subject only to an annual feudal fee of twenty pounds. It wasn't until 1587 that Halnaker House once again became the seat of an influential family when Elizabeth 1 sold the manor to John Morley, a wealthy merchant from Great Saxham in Suffolk. His family retained ownership of Halnaker and were patrons of the living at Boxgrove Priory for over 170 years until 1765. Once again the Manor House was to provide stability and work for a community upset by the changes instigated by Henry VIII.

The original house had been enriched and enlarged until by the end of the sixteenth century it must have been an extensive range of buildings with many gables, windows and chimneys. The buildings, which have been described in detail by F. W. Steer, were enclosed in an irregular quadrangle surrounded by huge walls. The striking gatehouse which can still be seen today was situated in the southern range of these walls and carried a portcullis. It is well preserved and gives a good indication of the house's former glory. Going into the courtyard from this gate you come upon smooth lawns and on the right hand side is the remains of the chapel, once a large building, about fifty five feet by twenty three feet, and of thirteenth century date. The walls are about three feet thick, and the remains of what could be a piscina are built into the blocked westernmost window on the south side. The altar is now the high altar in Boxgrove church.

The northern side of the quadrangle was occupied by the great house. Only traces remain today. Immediately to the right of the gatehouse was the great hall

Figure 24. The inner court of Halnaker House. From a drawing by S.H. Grimm, 1781.

Figure 25. The back part of Halnaker House, the well-shed, and other offices. From a drawing by William Bromet, 1840.

richly decorated with carved panelling by Lord De La Warr in about 1530 but of which only the east wall and a few feet of the south wall remain. Although little remains today of Robert De La Haye's original house, it is still worth taking a look at the ruins where, with a little imagination, one can picture the continuous bustle of a great household. For four hundred years it must have been not only the 'pretty house' described by Edward VI but large and impressive and, together with the Priory at Boxgrove, must have provided employment for many people living in the area.

The arrival of the Morleys brought to an end the unsatisfactory situation in which the Priory, now the parish church for Boxgrove and Halnaker, was without a parish priest. Since the death of the last vicar, Sir Thomas Boxfield, in 1548

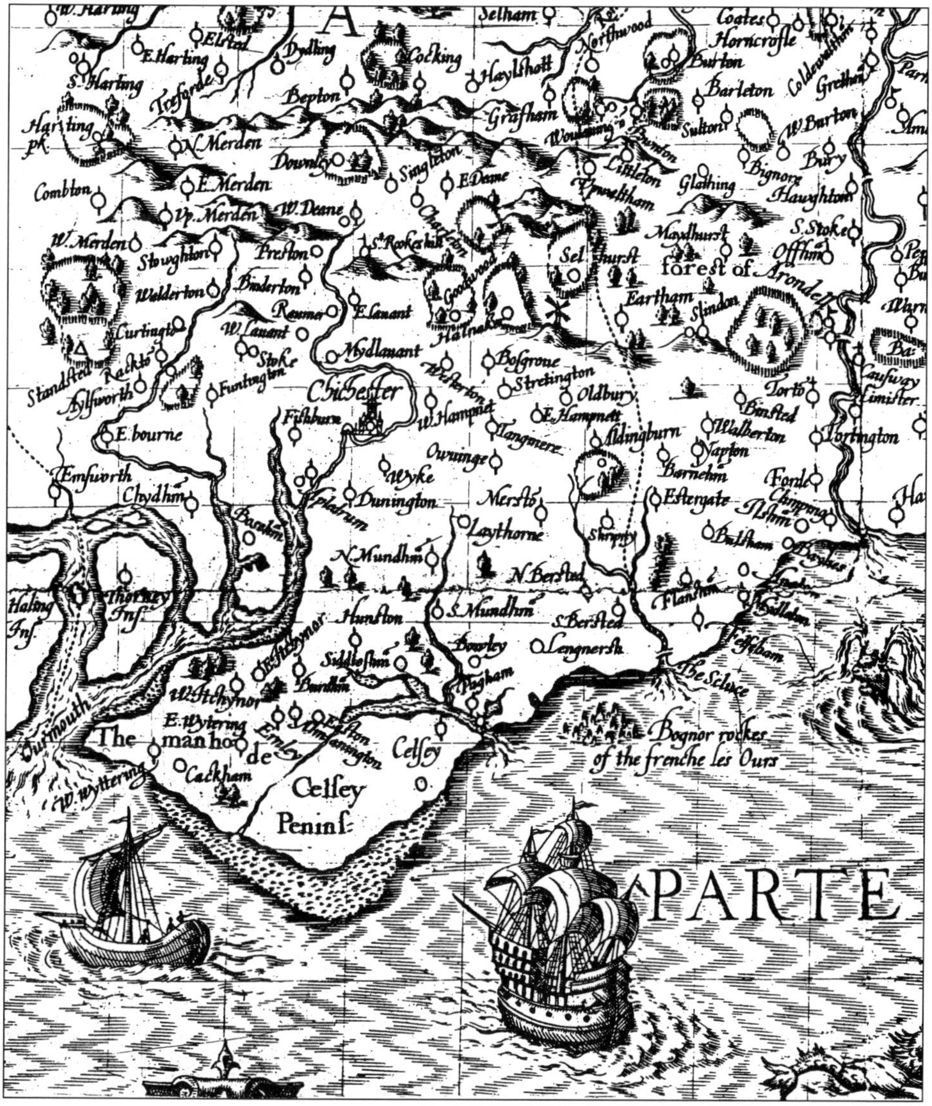

Figure 26. Detail from John Norden's map of Sussex dated 1595.

they had been managing with a series of curates, whilst the Crown appropriated almost all the relatively sizeable parish income. The diocesan records show, for instance, that, after one of the periodic visitations by the Bishop in 1563, it was reported that the Priory of Boxgrove had no vicar and no curate. In 1569 it is stated that 'In Boxgrove is a very fine church and there is neither parson, vicar nor curate, but a sorry reader, Sir Thomas Palmer, who is the farmer of the parsonage, as it is thought from the Erle of Arundell.'

Elsewhere in the Visitation it is hinted that Sir Thomas Palmer was papistically minded!

In 1577, when Henry Clerk was licensed curate, it was reported that there had been no vicar for thirty years. Not until 1581 was a vicar appointed, one John Hull, whose patron was Sir John Lumley, son-in-law of the Earl of Arundel and owner of Stansted House. He remained in office for sixteen years, and by then the vicars came under Morley patronage, and the community settled down to its parson and squire for the next three hundred years and will probably remain so for the next three hundred; the only difference being that the patronage had moved from Halnaker to Goodwood.

Figure 27. Sir John Morley. Print from painting – by Cornelius Johnson, 1631.

Despite the absence of a vicar for so long, the small community continued to sustain a constant congregation and also to find the necessary money to maintain the church. One can only suppose that it was the churchwardens who inspired parishioners to support their church in a practical way. It is also interesting to read how a number of legacies recorded in favour of the Priory enabled the churchwardens to maintain the fabric of the church. The number of these legacies increased from one or two per annum in the early fifteen hundreds, to eleven in 1557 and twelve in each of the years 1558 and 1559 under the patronage of the Earl of Arundel.

In 1612 John Morley, now Sir John Morley, appointed David Earle as vicar, the first university graduate in the history of the parish. From then on, under the Morley patronage, the academic backgrounds of the incumbents of the parish church were always impeccable, showing a bias in favour of the University of Cambridge.

The Morley family flourished at Halnaker acquiring knighthoods and intermarrying with local landowners. They are a good illustration of an upwardly mobile family which owed its prosperity to success in trade and its estates to the changes brought about by the Reformation. Many of the lands previously owned by monastic foundations were bought by people like the Morleys who now therefore had a vested interest in maintaining the status quo. They were a new breed of prosperous merchants conscious of their social standing in the county. The Morley coat-of-arms is an interesting illustration of how the family regarded themselves as heirs to those Norman knights who had built Halnaker House and lived there for four hundred years (see XVIII in colour section). The two leopards' heads spewing out fleurs-de-lis were the emblem of the Cantiloupe family, and the mullets which decorated the chevrons were the crests of the Bonvilles and St John families who had connections with Halnaker House before the Reformation. All these heraldic devices can be seen on the painted ceiling in the Priory church today, and it is interesting to note how the Morleys from Great Saxham in Suffolk made use of them when composing their own coat-of-arms. It must have given Sir William Morley, whose monument is in the north transept of the Priory, a great deal of satisfaction when his daughter, Mary, married James Stanley, Earl of Derby, on 7 February 1704 in the chapel of Halnaker House. Sir William had married the daughter of Sir Robert Heath, Chief Justice of the King's Bench, an interesting illustration of how far the Morley family had climbed socially in less than a hundred years.

One can picture the bustling activity that emanated from Halnaker House in the seventeenth century and the first half of the eighteenth: the dinner parties, the balls, the musical evenings, the hunts, providing work and excitement for the whole community. In the Morley archives we can read, with some amusement, how, in a letter of 1659, a Thomas Turner wrote to Edward Heath from Lady Morley's house in Halnaker about a debt of thirty shillings which Heath's nephew, John Morley, owed for a viol. In 1668 there is also a list of Lady Morley's debts, maybe the result of overspending brought about by the jubilation at Charles II's restoration.

Indeed Boxgrove and Halnaker did not escape disruption at the time of the Civil War. There is an interesting and entertaining entry in the Boxgrove Parish register from Samuel Hill, vicar between 1636-1663.

'Immediately after April 10th 1648 the Register bookes was unjustly taken from mee by Mr Cawley, the regicide, (as I was sequesterd by him from my Living before) and justly restored to mee again on 25 January 1660 by Mr Farrington, a Loyal Justice of Peace. In the meanetime (being thirteen years) it may appeare how confusedly, impertinently and preposterously things have been set down therein: and that many were omitted; yea, my very owne daughter next following was unregistered till now.' (The next entry is that of Mary, daughter of Samuel and Ann Hill, born 25 March, baptized 29 March 1649). In 1660 Hill, with a cry of triumph, writes 'Exit Registarius illegalis. Redit Vicarius legalis.' Things had returned to normal.

There is a previous entry in the parish register that, once again, raises a smile. In 1631 there is an entry by the curate that there was not enough wine on Easter Day. 'We wanted wine for a number of people' - a slip-up, no doubt, on the part of the church wardens!

Figure 29. James Stanley. 10th Earl of Derby 1664-1736
From an engraving by G Vander Gucht in 1734.

Squire and parson continued to support each other throughout the following centuries providing the typical social setting depicted by Jane Austen and other novelists. The Morleys would have driven down to the Parish Church on Sundays, sat in the family pew, surrounded by their tenants and retainers. Together they would have listened to the, no doubt, interminable sermons fashionable during the eighteenth century, had their children baptised there, attended weddings and funerals. Sometimes they left charitable bequests to the vicar. For instance, there is an indenture of 2 August 1704 between Mary Morley of Halnaker, Sussex, spinster, surviving daughter and heir of Sir William Morley KB, late of Halnaker, deceased, and others, of lands in trust to permit William Whitear, vicar of Boxgrove,... 'to enjoy the vicarage premises from Lady Day last for life, if he so long serves the cure of Boxgrove,.... thereafter to be put in trust for the new vicar.'

This would have given the vicar of Boxgrove a welcome increase in income as he would enjoy the rents from lands Mary Morley had settled on him and his heirs. It appears that the vicar of Boxgrove did rather well out of the bequests of

Figure 28. Detail from a map by Richard Budgen 1724.

the charitable ladies. There is an interesting record that Lady Hyde left instructions to pay the vicar of Boxgrove forty shillings annually for preaching four sermons a year in Boxgrove church. There is also a note that the sermon on the 30 June was deemed not worth observing and that the ten shillings be given away in bread for the poor of the parish!

Despite the patronage of the squire it is interesting to read in the reports of the diocesan inspectors of the time that the parish church of Boxgrove showed no great improvement in the state of its fabric and its church services. No doubt this is a reflection of the general state of the Church of England in the early eighteenth century rather than a criticism of the Halnaker patrons. In 1724 there was a Visitation by the Diocese of Chichester to Boxgrove Priory in which it was reported; 'We gather that the state of the fabrics and of their fittings was in many places just as bad as it had been forty years before. There was one service or sermon on Sundays, and the administration of the Holy Communion four times a year'. The bishops were probably well content if they could secure as much as this. As to the state of the church fabric, most reports today on the same subject would probably say the same thing.

Undoubtedly the star of the Morley family was Mary, Countess of Derby, whose body is buried in St John's chapel in the Priory, and whose monument, in the North transept, is one of the best artistic features in the Priory. Sir William Morley's daughter, Mary, married James Stanley, tenth Earl of Derby in 1704 in the chapel of Halnaker House. William Morley left Halnaker to Mary, who, after

Figure 30. Memorial to Mary, Countess of Derby in Boxgrove Priory

her husband's death, returned to Halnaker and devoted herself to good works. The impressive monument in the Priory, carved out of ivory, shows Mary, draped in classical costume, sitting under an oak tree dispensing alms to a family similarly attired. Underneath the monument there is an inscription which reads:

'To the memory of the Right Honourable Mary, Countess Dowager of Derby, daughter and heiress of Sir William Morley of Halnaker, Knight of the Bath, and relict of James, Earl of Derby, by whom she had issue, William, Lord Strange, who died young.

'Her calmness and patience in adversity were as exemplary as her humility and moderation in prosperity. Her temper remarkably even and cheerful. She was adorned with every Christian grace and virtue. Her charity was universal, witness her extensive benefactions to this and other neighbouring parishes, illustrious and lasting monument of her munificence. Such was the influence of a lively faith and the overflowing of a benevolent heart that she made it the sole business, as it was the chief pleasure of her life, to serve God and do good. She died on 28 March 1752 in the 85th year of her age and was buried in the opposite vault.'

When Mary died in 1752 she left Halnaker House in her will to her cousin, Sir Thomas Dyke Acland who, in 1765, sold it to Charles, Third Duke of Richmond, who owned the neighbouring Goodwood House. The Duke became the patron of the Priory and Chairman of the Trustees for Mary's almshouses, positions that his heirs still occupy today. The Duke's interest in Halnaker seems to have been mainly in the estate for the house was left empty and by 1804 had become a ruin, it's fabric removed piece by piece to embellish houses in Chichester and even for road repair.

One of Mary's good works, when she returned to Halnaker, had been to set up almshouses for the relief of poor women. These almshouses are still standing today, and the people living in them form a lively and useful community. On the front of the almshouses, which are situated next to the school which Mary also founded, there is a plaque bearing these words. 'These buildings were erected and endowed by the Right Honourable Mary, Countess of Derby, daughter and heiress of Sir William Morley late of Halnaker, Knight of the Honourable Order of the Bath'.

In the Chichester Record Office there is the indenture of bargain and sale, dated 2 January 1740, duly enrolled in the Court of Chancery on 13 February 1740 between the Rt. Hon. Mary Countess of Derby, John Verney Esq., Master of the Rolls, and four others of the other part. Then to quote: 'the said Countess granted to the parties of the second part a piece of ground containing by estimation 1 acre (more or less) called Mary's garden, lying on the west side of Boxgrove Street, in trust to them and their heirs for ever.'

She set aside an annuity, in trust, for the purpose of building the almshouses. It should be spent 'to lay out the same (i.e. the land set aside) in erecting such almshouses on the said plot of ground as the trustees, with the approbation of the said Countess, her heirs or assigns, should deem meet, for the habitation of a schoolmaster and 12 poor widows or maidens, apportioning the remainder of the said plot for gardens, to be enjoyed with such separate habitations respectively, and in fencing the said garden.'

As well as setting up the almshouses there is in the instruction to set up a school: 'That the said trustees should settle in the said dwellings a sufficiently qualified schoolmaster, of the Communion of the Church of England and a frequenter of the said church, for the teaching of twelve poor boys or girls in reading, writing and arithmetic; and twelve poor widows or aged maidens of the communion of the said church and being of good report, and settled inhabitants of and within the parishes of Boxgrove, East Lavant and Tangmere, six poor widows or maidens of the said parish of Boxgrove, four of East Lavant and two of Tangmere.'

Also there are instructions that the schoolmaster should be paid £15 per annum, and the said widow or maiden who should assist him 'as should be qualified for teaching of the said poor children in reading and needlework', £10 per annum. To each of the poor widows or maidens £9 per annum, and £1 a year for fuel. 'The said several payments to be made at Lady Day and Michaelmas half yearly.'

Money was also to be held in trust for clothing for the twelve boys or girls. Mary was essentially a practical lady.

From time to time the occupants of the almshouses had to sign a declaration that they would behave themselves, and there is one such document, called 'Declarations', made by the occupants of the almshouses between 1844-1859 which gives us a good insight into the minds of the Trustees of such institutions. It is worth quoting the document in full:

'The following Rules and Regulations are ordered to be observed by the inmates of the Countess of Derby's Almshouse at Boxgrove.

1. It is ordered that every inmate of the Almshouses shall attend Divine Service at the Parish Church as often as the means and opportunity of doing so shall be offered to her, provided she be not otherwise hindered by sickness or bodily infirmity.

2. That no inmate shall allow any son or other male relation or friend to sleep in her apartments on any pretence whatsoever, nor any daughter or other female relative or friend, without the express permission of the Minister of the Parish.
3. That no spirituous liquor of any kind be allowed to be taken into any apartment unless ordered by a medical attendant.
4. That any inmate who shall be accused of Felony, Blasphemy, Slandering, Brawling, Disorderly conduct of any kind, or a breach of any of the above rules, shall, if summoned, appear before a Meeting of the Trustees to answer such charge and, provided such charge shall be proved to the satisfaction of the trustees so assembled, such inmate shall be liable to such punishment, whether it be censure, fine or dismissed from the rights and privileges to which she became entitled upon her election - as the Trustees shall determine and think fit to award.
5. Every person who shall, from and after this date, be elected shall sign a paper to the following effect. "I, A.B. having been elected to an apartment in Lady Derby's Almshouses in the Parish of Boxgrove, do hereby agree to observe all the Rules and Regulations which have been, or shall hereafter, be made by the Trustees of the charity, for the well ordering and good government of the society, of which I have now become a member."

Signed C.D.

Note - a copy of the above rules to be read over to each one desirous of being recommended for election, and no election shall be considered valid until the person elected shall have signed the above declaration.

Signed by the Order of the Trustees.
Richmond, Etc. Chairman
Boxgrove, February 25th 1844'

It is interesting to note that, of all the occupants of the almshouses at that time, only four ladies, Phoebe Dewry, Martha Prinstead, Hannah Smith and Louisa Howard, could sign their names. The others signed with a cross and each cross is different.

Each of the ladies lived in her own little house with an outside privy (now converted into garden sheds). Twenty six years ago the building was converted into flats and only four years ago the modern top floor was added to the building. The present warden lives in the top flat. Nowadays twenty residents occupy these warm and cosy dwellings and make up a peaceful and cheerful community. The gardens at the rear of the buildings are beautifully cared for. In summer they are bright with flowers and abundant with vegetables.

The Countess of Derby's benefaction, in 1740, provided for the support of a schoolmaster, the education and clothing of twelve poor children from Boxgrove, East Lavant and Tangmere, as well as the support of the inhabitants of the almshouses. At first the school was situated at the front of the almshouses, the schoolmaster's house being at the back where today there is the entrance to the warden's flat. From the school records we gather that the school flourished during the nineteenth century, and at the Diocesan Inspection of September 1906 the Inspector, Hugh Horden, noted that 'The teaching is sound and thorough and there is a good manly tone among the boys. They know their work very well and passed a very creditable examination'. Hugh Horden was the Inspector for several years in the early part of the twentieth century and not only was academic knowledge commented upon, but also the children's physical appearance. For instance, in July 1910 one of the boys, Ernest McCarthy, was reported to be 'very thin and pale. He should have plenty of fresh milk daily and fresh air'.

In 1868 the girls' school was housed in a new building, 'built by his Grace the Duke of Richmond and Gordon' and the girls moved in on 7 June of that year. The boys remained in the schoolroom at the front of the almshouses until 1915 when the girls' school was enlarged and provided accommodation for both boys and girls. The present school occupies the 1868 girls' school building, but it has been extended and modernised over the years. The girls' school Log Book is in the Chichester Record Office. It contains some fascinating information and has provided us with a good insight into the life of the times.

For instance, epidemics could cause havoc with the school time table, and there is an entry in the Log Book that on 25 September 1877 the school was closed due to an outbreak of scarlet fever. The school was closed for six weeks. Also in 1892 the school was closed for three months because of an outbreak of measles, a killer in the days before immunisation. Scarlet fever, whooping cough and diphtheria were the deadly plagues of childhood in the last century and the early part of the twentieth.

The school was regularly inspected and the reports of the inspectors are very revealing. The girls seemed to be extraordinarily good at needlework, a tradition that lasted well into the twentieth century. Ladies who attended the school in the nineteen thirties, describe how the old boys' school, at the front of the almshouses, accommodated a loom and on this loom the material was woven for two skirts for the Queen Mother, then Duchess of York, in 1934. They were made of heather coloured tweed and the ladies remember the excitement when the material was taken to Windsor Castle.

Unfortunately arithmetic and writing were not strong points in the girls performance. Nor was the Inspector satisfied with the way they were taught, and there are entries in the reports where it is recommended that one of the teachers should be removed. Several times the school grant was cut because the children were below standard.

No doubt both boys and girls were on their best behaviour when the Diocesan Inspector came on his visits, and the vicar was a frequent and well-known figure at the school. The day always started with prayers. Children went to church on Sunday and to Sunday school, where they were taught the essentials of the Christian Faith. There are several reports in the Log Book where girls had been reprimanded for behaving badly in church. Several times they were kept in after school for the same offence.

Browsing through the parish magazines of that time, the late nineteenth century and the early years of the twentieth, there is a clear picture of the village united under it's squire and vicar. The Duke of Richmond at Goodwood House owned much of the property in the village and was also Chairman of the Trustees for the Countess of Derby's Almshouses and her school, whilst the vicar, of course, took a full part in the everyday life of the parish. There were holidays linked to the major church festivals, such as Ascension Day, when the children took part in sports and feasts provided by the 'big house' and supported by the parish. Children could come and go safely in a parish where everyone was known and where there was little privacy, but comforting security. Children went to school at the age of five and stayed until fourteen, when the headmaster acted as a Job Centre and found them work. The girls most often went to the big houses in the area where they were employed as domestic servants and the boys found work on the land. We know it wasn't idyllic; the entries in the Log Book about poor attendance due to illness, and the school closures due to epidemics show this, but the children felt safe and loved in a community that was almost an extended family. All this was to change during the Second World War.

Mary, Countess of Derby, would have been well pleased if she could have seen the results of her benefactions. The almshouses provided safe housing for the poor women of Boxgrove and neighbouring parishes, and the school gave a solid grounding in the three 'R's' for two hundred years, and continues to provide excellent education today. The children in their royal blue pullovers are a much loved part of the present community.

CRICKET AT BOXGROVE

Illustrations of bat and ball games are seen in medieval manuscripts and from these early forms of cricket modern cricket has developed.

In 1622 a game of cricket was played in the churchyard at Boxgrove and the following account is based upon the researches of Timothy McCann and Peter Wilkinson as reported in the Sussex Archaeological Collections.

Figure 31. 'A Game of Cricket' (c. 1340)

This is not the earliest mention of the word cricket, or even the earliest recorded mention of people playing cricket. It is important, however, as the earliest recorded instance so far discovered, of a game of cricket played by several named players, in Sussex, or, for that matter, anywhere else. The record of the game was first discovered by Dr Hilda Johnstone when editing a volume of Churchwardens Presentments and it has been written about frequently since that date. However, recent research among the records of the Consistory Court at Chichester has brought to light fresh documentary evidence about the game.

On Sunday, 28 April, 1622, Anthony Ward, servant to Daniel Earle, the vicar of Boxgrove, and Edward Hartley, played cricket together during the time of Evensong. On the following Sunday, 5 May, Edward Hartley together with Raphe West, Richard Slaughter, William Martin, Richard Martin junior, and others whose names were not recorded, played another game in the churchyard at Boxgrove, and were aided and abetted in so doing by Richard Martin senior and Thomas West, the two churchwardens of the parish. As a result of these two games, the participants were presented by the new churchwardens in their Easter Bills. Unfortunately, the original churchwardens' presentment for 1622 has not survived, but a record of it was written into a contemporary register of presentments. Under the heading of Easter Bills for 1622, the entry for Boxgrove reads:- 'I present Raphe West, Edward Hartley, Richard Slaughter, William Martin, Richard Martin junior, together with others in theire company whose names I have no notice of, for playing at crecket in the churchyard on Sunday, the fifte of May, after sufficient warning given to the contrary, for three speciall reasons: first, for that it is contrary to the 7th article; secondly, for that they use to breake the Church-windowes with the ball; and thirdly, for that a little childe had like to have her braynes beaten out with a cricket batt. And also I present Richard Martin senior and Thomas West the old churchwardens for defending and mayntayning them in it.... Wee present Anthony Ward, servant to Mr Earle, our minister, and Edward Hartley, for playing at creket in the evening prayer tyme on Sunday the xxviij th of Aprill.'

Following their presentment, the cricketers were cited to appear before the Consistory Court in Chichester Cathedral and having pleaded guilty were dismissed with a pious admonition.

The procedure must have been sufficiently unpleasant to make the players wary of a future game. It involved a four mile journey from Boxgrove to Chichester, and more important, probably the loss of a whole day's work. There in the Cathedral they had to endure fairly ignominious treatment of both their self esteem and their pocket. First came the public confession. This would involve each of the men reciting in open court a suitably penitent statement of their offence and their repentance. They were then admonished by the judge - on this occasion the Bishop himself. This must have given the occasion a greater sense of gravity than might be expected, for during this period most of the courts were conducted neither by the Bishop himself nor his commissary, but by a more lowly surrogate. Bishop Carleton was perhaps rather exceptional in presiding at a number of the sittings of his court at this time; and in detection cases where the role of the judge was frequently to deliver a moral lecture rather than a legal judgement, his presence must have added considerably to the efficacy of the sentence.

Finally came the fees. Opposite the name of each offender in the Detection Book the scribe has scribbled the figure xiid presumably the amount extracted for the court's expenses. Although this might not seem too formidable a sum to the husbandmen among the players, it would be a fairly crippling sum for a mere servant like Ward.

Other contemporary records give us an idea of the age and social standing of the players. The baptism entries in Boxgrove parish register at least suggest that the game was more than a schoolboy lark in the churchyard; for Ralph West was christened in 1588. William Martin in 1594 and Richard Martin junior in 1606. The register, together with the wills proved in the Chichester ecclesiastical courts also show why the old churchwardens defended and maintained them in the game, for the three players we have mentioned prove to be their sons. This in turn sheds an interesting light on their social status, for churchwardens had to be at least respectable householders. In their wills both Thomas West and Richard Martin senior describe themselves as husbandmen, which would suggest they were probably tenant farmers. Their probate inventories show that they both lived in similar six-roomed houses, and each left personal estate valued at £89 - quite a substantial sum. Ironically, one of them seems, before the game, to have been on friendly or even intimate terms with the vicar Daniel Earle. Two depositions in the church court indicate that in 1612 Richard Martin senior and Earle had been summoned together to the bedside of a dying parishioner, while his will, made only three months before the game, names his 'well beloved friend' Earle as his overseer.

Finally, there are three points of interest about the presentment itself. First, that playing cricket was considered to be contrary to the 7th Article. When they were preparing their Easter Bills, the churchwardens would, presumably, refer to a set of Visitation Articles, which must have provided them with a general framework for making presentments even when they were not actually making their return at a Visitation. Unfortunately, no articles for 1621 or 1622 appear to have survived, but those administered by Bishop Montague in 1628, throw an interesting light on the affair. In the section headed, 'Articles concerning the Church, the Ornaments, sacred utensills, and possessions of the same,' the 7th article reads, 'Whether is your churchyard well mounded, and fenced, kept cleane without Nusance, or soyle cast into it; is it incroached uppon, and by whome; doe any offensively keepe doores, outletts, or passages into your churchyard: doe any use to quarrell, fight, play or make meetings, banquets, Church-ales there, doe any keepe Courts, Leetes, Lawdaies, Musters there, or otherwise use it being a consecrated place, prophaned contrarie to the 88 Canon.'

Secondly, the fact that there was a danger of breaking the windows of the church suggests that some sort of hard ball was used for the game. Several writers have remarked on the third point - the reason why the little child was in danger of having her brains beaten out with a cricket bat. Both Rowland Bowen and R. F. Hunnisett have suggested that the rules under which the game was then played, allowed the batsman to hit the ball twice, not just if he was in danger of being dismissed, but also for his 'general advantage.' Certainly the West Hoathly inquest on Jaspar Vinall who was killed after being struck on the head by Edward Tye, who was playing cricket with him, in 1624, and the death of Henry Brand of Selsey from a similar injury in 1647 powerfully support this argument.

Figure 32. Charles Lennox, 2nd Duke of Richmond 1701 – 1750.

By 1730 competitive cricket was thriving in West Sussex. Boxgrove being situated between the great names of Slindon and Goodwood it is very likely that local residents were involved in the game. John Marshall in his book 'Sussex Cricket' describes the scene. Richard Newland, a Chichester surgeon, who has been called the 'father of cricket' lived at Slindon where he lead a team which became one of the strongest in the country, challenging London and even county sides. At the end of 1741 they could claim that only once in 43 matches had they been defeated. Newland captained All-England and was probably the greatest all rounder of his day (see XXIII in colour section).

The second Duke of Richmond was also a great enthusiast for the game and had large responsibility for the establishment of organised cricket in Sussex. On his estate at Goodwood he employed as grooms, gardeners, etc. some of the best players of the day who were thus almost professionals. One such was Thomas Waymark who played for Sussex and for All-England. There is a record of a cricket match played at Halnaker in 1749 in which the Duke of Richmond's sons took part with local players and where the umpire was 'Thomas Waymark, whom the Duke formerly kept to play cricket'.

The village under the patronage of Goodwood was, thus closely involved in cricket and this must have continued, for the 3rd Duke of Richmond was captain of Sussex and his son founded the M.C.C.

THE ASCENDANCY OF GOODWOOD

As has been previously illustrated, Boxgrove village had traditionally fallen under the patronage and control of the family resident in Halnaker House. This heritage continued well into the eighteenth century under the Morley family, their estate passing finally to a distant cousin Sir Thomas Dyke Acland in 1752, there being no direct heirs. Sir Thomas spent little time in Halnaker, possessing his own property elsewhere, so for a period the village lacked the presence and support of a constantly resident squire.

There had however been another family of stature resident in the parish since 1695, when Charles Lennox, the first Duke of Richmond (an illegitimate son of Charles II) bought a 200 acre estate at Goodwood. On the estate was a house described as a hunting lodge, lying within the parish boundaries but somewhat distant from the actual village. The second Duke developed the property to become the family's country seat, and took advantage of the situation to enlarge his holding by purchasing the Halnaker House estate in 1765. His successors have of course remained in constant occupation without interruption up to the present time.

The immediate consequence of this change of ownership was that Boxgrove village found itself completely enclosed on all sides by one estate, and its subsequent development remained that of a closed village until well into the twentieth century. The Gordon-Lennox family continued to expand the area of the estate progressively until around 1850, whilst the third Duke (see XIX in colour section) replaced the original hunting lodge with the handsome mansion and imposing stable block which we see today. It is of interest that immediately after acquiring the Halnaker lands the family took steps to have the main Chichester Petworth road diverted to its present line along the Roman Stane Street, thus avoiding the annoyance of having the home park divided by a public highway.

The Lennox family appear from the beginning to have been substantially disinterested in the fine house at Halnaker, and progressively allowed it to fall into ruin. It is known that some of the stone was subsequently sold for building purposes elsewhere, and in fact two of the fine windows still survive in one of the houses in the Chichester Cathedral Close, The Chantry.

By 1850 the Goodwood estate had reached what was to be its maximum size

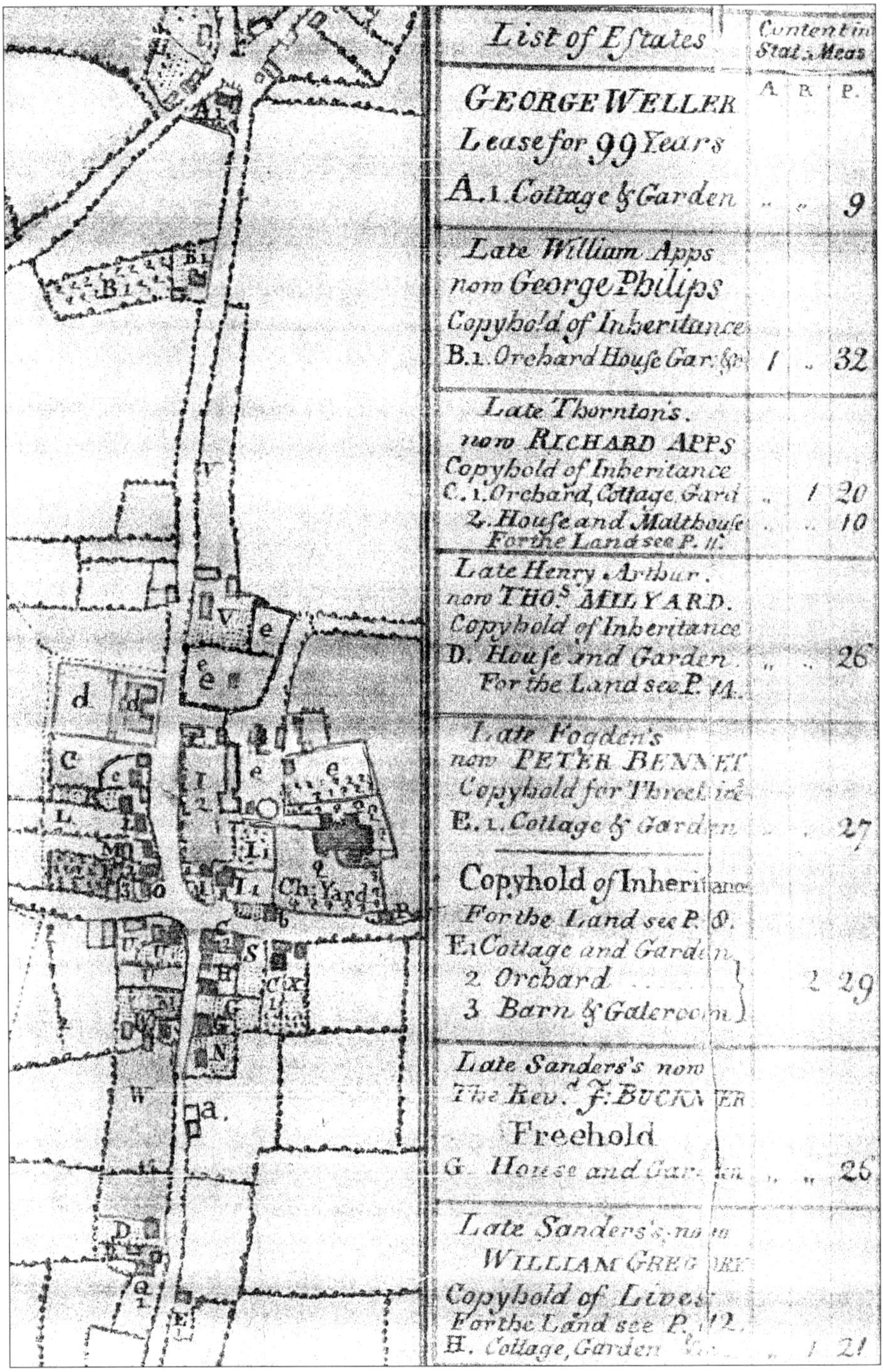

Figure 33. Detail from a map of Boxgrove in 1781 with a table of occupancy, by Yeakell and Gardiner. Reproduced by courtesy of the Trustees of the Goodwood Estate.

of 17,000 acres, stretching from the parish of Bosham on the coast to East Dean on the north side of the Downs. In consequence estate workers cottages were not confined to Boxgrove, but scattered over this wider area, so that Boxgrove village remained virtually static in size and proportion for some two hundred years. We are able to trace this aspect in some detail subsequent to the first official census in 1801, and the table below demonstrates that the village population reached its peak of 868 in 1821, a figure never exceeded until the population pattern in West Sussex changed dramatically with the massive influx of retirement age residents after the 1939/45 war. It is of interest that five other villages lying within the boundaries of the Goodwood Estate and Chichester Rape have shown an almost identical population pattern.

	Population	No. of Houses/Dwellings
1801	682	151
1811	754	-
1821	868	152
1831	778	153
1841	736	147
1851	755	151
1861	666	158
1871	728	165
1881	708	155
1891	690	162
1901	651	161
1911	610	167
1921	621	160
1931	681	169

By 1961, however, the population had increased by 49% to 1018, with 39 additional dwellings.

Although it was never the case that the village was exclusively inhabited by Goodwood Estate staff, there is no doubt that the majority of its inhabitants were economically dependant upon it for their livelihood. The census of 1821 showed that of the 167 resident families, 131 worked in agriculture, 25 in trade and only 11 in other professions. It would appear also that a relatively high proportion of families remained settled in the village, the 1851 census showing that 42% of those classified as labourers had been born in the parish, as had 51% of the artisans. The same census showed however that only 19% of the

Goodwood House staff were of local origin – a reflection perhaps of a low standard of education and culture amongst the cottagers.

We must note therefore that throughout a fairly long period, from 1765 to 1918, the village remained almost static in size. Conditions for the working class (normally described as cottagers) were hard, as throughout the whole period reviewed in this chapter, the village had no running water, public sanitation, refuse collection, electricity or gas. The local roads were recognised as being in poor condition, and any villager wanting to go even as far as Chichester had to walk or arrange a lift with the carter who served the little community. Most of the agricultural labourers worked on the local farms as casual workers, which at times exposed them to considerable hardship – a few fortunate exceptions being the permanent forestry workers attached to what was then a sizeable Goodwood estate enterprise.

In these circumstances, the villagers undoubtedly developed a strong community spirit helped by the active leadership of two institutions – the Goodwood Estate and the parish church, Boxgrove Priory

The influence and role of the Church changed in form very considerably throughout the 150 years from 1750, but it was always a dominant factor in the life of the village. It has to be remembered that in the seventeenth century it had been, at least in theory, a legal obligation to attend Sunday service in one's parish church, and that people were subject to a church court system running in parallel to the civil courts. Church courts concentrated in practice on problems of social behaviour in a community, matters affecting the Church (e.g. attendance failures, tithes, etc.), and they also had a great influence on family matters arising from handling a high proportion of will probates, for which they were considered more efficient and less costly than the crown courts.

An illustration of the type of charges brought before the church courts is to be found in two cases brought by the Boxgrove church wardens in 1622 and 1623. The first of these was against a couple for promiscuity, the wife being pregnant before the wedding ceremony, and the second against a female villager for 'abusing the minister in abusive and irreverent speeches, saying that he was a drunken and whoremaster priest.' Although these church courts could only impose fines, public admonitions or excommunication, a presentation of this nature was an effective form of discipline up to a point, as it would involve losing a day's work to attend the hearing in Chichester, and also, at a minimum, having to pay the legal costs of the hearing.

Boxgrove remained, of course, essentially an agricultural and rural village until after the First World War, and it is in this respect that the policies of the Gordon-Lennox family had the most continuous and lasting influence on this small community.

The family's style of management was essentially paternalistic, maintaining a close local contact with all classes of society, and as being constant benefactors in their support of the church, village, schools, hospitals and cases of individual misfortune. The fourth Duke between 1764 and 1819, in fact, went so far as to

Figure 34. Boxgrove Priory in 1772.

set aside a part of his day so that any local resident could seek an audience. The effectiveness of such active paternalism was proved in November 1830 when, in a period of deep depression, there were agricultural riots in Sussex. Some 200 labourers were threatening violence, whereupon the Duke was able to muster a force of 50 tenant farmers to confront them. But the force of his personality and his reputation sufficed to persuade all concerned to avoid violence and indeed to depart in good humour.

Apart from the Home Farm adjacent to Boxgrove, most of the estate was placed in the hands of tenant farmers and the traditional social pattern of titled landlords, large and medium yeomen, with only some 0.4% of land owned by cottagers, was maintained until the end of the nineteenth century. The fact that it was possible to maintain this social pyramid virtually unchanged was by that date exceptional in England, and must be attributed to the flexibility with which the family administered their policies. They had a merited reputation for paying extremely low wages, but the villagers did not forget, for instance, that in 1852 in a period of extreme economic difficulty, they permitted 63 cottagers to delay paying their rents, and, the malaise continuing, excused them from this debt entirely in 1853.

Successive Dukes had the reputation of being leaders in agriculture, the fifth and sixth being each in their turn Presidents of the Royal Agricultural Society, and leading speakers in the House of Lords on all matters affecting the agricultural industry. They expected their tenant farmers to follow their progressive new farming techniques, and the pattern of agriculture surrounding Boxgrove village even today must be considered a direct legacy of their estate management policies. Infinite patience was shown to receptive, hard working and morally sound tenants, but whenever a family fell below the desired standard in any respect they would be forced to quit their house and, in most cases, the opportunity would be seized to amalgamate a property with a neighbouring farm and obtain the economic benefits of size. As a result the smaller farms progressively disappeared, and today Boxgrove is entirely surrounded by farming units of a very considerable size.

In one other respect, moreover, the Goodwood estate policies affected a much wider area than their own acreage. During the period 1839–1864, when the majority of railway lines were built in England, the fifth Duke was consistently opposed to permitting any such constructions to impinge upon his land. As a result Chichester never benefited from a direct railway line to London, and lost its economic status as one of the largest towns in the southern region. The effect on the town was, indeed, dramatic its population remaining virtually static until 1921, whilst over the same period Brighton virtually tripled in size.

Throughout the eighteenth and nineteenth centuries successive Dukes were numbered amongst the leading sportsmen in England, and their commitment brought considerable activity to Boxgrove. Cricket expanded as a sport in its early days due to large landowners sponsoring and organising their own teams, which then played challenge matches. These were important local events and allowed the opportunity for large wagers. The third Duke of Richmond was amongst the leading enthusiasts, providing employment amongst his estate staff for gifted players. Timothy McCann, at the County Record Office, has written an extensive paper on a match of this type, played in 1741, when the Duke took advantage of an occasion when all the local gentry and larger yeomen farmers were assembled in one spot to spend the day lining up support for his favoured candidate at a local by-election. It was an operation he described in a letter to the 'First Minister' of the day, the Duke of Newcastle, as having been entirely successful.

The Richmond family's devotion to sport of all forms also provided considerable employment in the district, and kept it well in the public eye. In 1730 the same Duke had become the sole owner and Master at the Charlton Hunt, whose reputation he built up until it became regarded as the first in England

Later Dukes built up Goodwood Race Course to become one of the most fashionable in the country, and it is on record that the need for casual labour to prepare the course and run it during a meeting, became, with time, a substantial form of alternative employment for the casual labourers of Boxgrove (see XX and XXI in colour section).

As we move into the nineteenth century the role of the church moved from being a centre of blind faith and social discipline into the very Victorian concept of positive and practical leadership coupled with a sense of responsibility for the less fortunate brethren. In this sense the church, and equally importantly the vicarage, became the social centre of the village in almost every respect, at least until the construction of a village club in the nineteen twenties.

The religious census of 1851 showed the average attendance at morning service was some 250 adults, with a further 150 at evensong. In addition the Sunday School had some 59 children attending - overall a significant proportion of the small village population.

The vicar served as advisor to the cottagers and assumed responsibility for managing the village school as Chairman of the Governors. It is significant that the first village magazine (1892) was the creation of a temporary curate, and successive vicars continued thereafter as editors and de facto publishers at least until the retirement of Father Popham in1957.

The magazine gives a fascinating insight into life in the village in the Victorian era. One can appreciate the importance of the activities organised by the vicar's wife and, through the vicarage, the constant and benevolent support of the Gordon-Lennox family, and the sense of social responsibility shown by the relatively few other local families of gentry status, towards those residents bluntly described as 'the poor'.

The vicar's wife organised and ran a branch of the Girls' Friendly Society, an organisation basically trying to provide some form of social activity and moral guidance for the many young girls living away from home, as domestic servants in the houses of the gentry and larger tenant farmers. She also organised and ran a village lending library, (subscription 2/6d per year but only 1/- for labourers), and organised social events for the members of the choir and church servers.

Figure 35. Interior of Boxgrove Church in 1833.

The Duke provided a club room in the village, decorated and maintained by estate workers, so that the younger men could have a social centre in the evenings, apart from the public house, and he provided it with newspapers and other periodicals. There was a village Medical Society, largely subsidised by the Gordon-Lennox family, which provided a resident village nurse and a doctor's weekly consultation surgery. There was a published scale of fees (daily visits 2/6d per week, night nursing 1/1d per night) but also a clear statement that the service was free for 'the poor.' A Captain Wilson for many years laid on a children's party in his home specifically confined to the children of the poor families, so that they should not feel excluded from the festivities. The club house served also as a centre for courses in carpentry, needlework and health education.

There were two village schools, one for each sex, essentially church institutions, deriving from the legacy of the Countess of Derby. The education offered was relatively minimal as, until the Education Act of 1894, children had only been obliged to attend up to the age of ten. School attendance then became compulsory up to the age of thirteen, but a pupil could still leave at eleven provided the minimum standard requirement had been achieved. The Parish Magazine frequently reported periods of several weeks when the schools had to be closed owing to the severity of the whooping cough or scarlet fever epidemics ravaging the village - a situation that was accepted as normal by the government inspectors. It was as late as 1903 before the County Council accepted responsibility for providing education in the village.

The community was obviously fond of organising concert evenings, usually to aid some village cause, at which a number of local musicians, singers and amateur comedians appeared only too willing to perform - all of whose efforts were faithfully reported in the magazine. It is worth noting that these social occasions seemed especially popular if they could be combined with dancing.

The Local Government Act of 1894 saw the creation of the first Parish Council, which duly elected the Duke of Richmond as its first chairman on 13 December that year. Initially it had little opportunity to be a really active body. The minutes for the first few years of its existence report meetings held to comply with the legal requirement of the Act and promptly adjourned 'there being no other business'.

The extensive restoration of the Priory between 1860 and 1865 affords a clear demonstration of the manner in which the village's affairs were managed in practice. In 1860 there was clear indication that both the roof and the flying buttresses were in very poor state, and the Vestry Minutes over the next two years show a considerable reluctance to face up to the financial implications of the problem. Eventually this body was forced to authorise a complete professional survey of the building, which indicated that unless considerable works were undertaken quite urgently the building might well collapse. The Vestry finally committed itself to some £450 of expenditure on the structural repairs, which had the effect of raising the Church Rate from 6d to 1/3d in the pound. Nowhere in its minutes, however, is there mention of the refurbishment of the interior of the church undertaken by Sir Gilbert Scott, at the initiation of the Duke, involving the removal of the flagstone floor, the insertion of the wooden pews, a tiled floor and a primitive heating system. It is reliably reported that the Duke's personal expenditure in this respect was in excess of £3,500. There was undoubtedly much background discussion over the proposed changes. Sir Gilbert's suggestion that the painted ceiling be removed as 'inappropriate in a House of God' was not accepted, but the Duke felt obliged to concede that the Chantry Chapel be restored to its original form, and not continue as a curtained snuggery in which his family could follow services in warmth and privacy.

The pattern of village life continued almost unchanged until the outbreak of war in 1914. A large proportion of the younger men disappeared into the forces, but the villagers were gratified in that local service units adopted the practice of marching their men to morning service in the Priory as a suitable form of Church Parade. Seventeen of the village's sons failed to return and are duly remembered on the war memorial in the Priory, but its social structure is faithfully reflected in the fact that all but one of them who fell were other ranks, the sole officer casualty being a Gordon-Lennox.

THE CHARLTON HUNT

The 17th century saw the development of a number of famous hunts, generally founded, financed and controlled by some large landowner. In West Sussex the Duke of Monmouth and Lord Grey of Uppark House (later created Earl of Tankerville) started such a hunt around 1675, basing the hounds variously during the season at Charlton or Uppark. Their huntsmen provided excellent sport, and it rapidly became a recognised meeting point for aristocratic hunting enthusiasts. The hunt members wore a distinctive livery of blue and silver.

Charlton, itself, was a small village of some remoteness in those days which meant that the hunt supporters found themselves obliged to stay in the vicinity for several days at a time. Many built their own hunting boxes in the village to avoid the difficulty of finding lodgings, and by 1720 it was such a popular venue that a subscription was raised amongst the followers to finance the building of a banqueting room so that they might have the opportunity to meet at dinner in the evenings. The aristocratic nature of this group may be judged by the fact that amongst these subscribers were two dukes, two marquises and five earls. This building (popularly called Fox Hall) is preserved today in Charlton by the Landmark Trust.

The second Duke of Richmond became, in time, closely involved in the Charlton Hunt, becoming joint master in 1728, and proprietor and sole master in 1730. In that year he also succeeded in extending the family estate into the heartland of the Hunt when he was able to purchase the manors at Singleton and Charlton. From that moment the Hunt kennels were established solely in Charlton.

The Richmond hunting box in the village was completed by 1732, by which date other part time recruits included the Dukes of Grafton and Devonshire, the Earl of Halifax, and the Lords De La Warr, Walpole and Harcourt. By 1738 the Hunt had become so popular that it was considered necessary to limit numbers by transforming it into a club, election to which was necessary before one was allowed to follow the hounds. At any one time over 100 horses would be stabled in the village, and the hunt club appointed a head groom to control the numerous stable staff involved. The village grew to considerable size, and in addition to the area in which the majority of the aristocratic hunting boxes had been built there was also a section centred around a low life public house, frequented by the grooms and domestic staff, which acquired quite a dubious reputation.

In all this activity the Duke of Richmond was the leading spirit. He had, of course, considerable political responsibilities, and in the well documented correspondence which he maintained with a leading politician of the day, the Duke of Newcastle, it is amusing to observe one constant theme as he explains the impossibility of his being in London on certain important dates.

The second Duke of Richmond died somewhat suddenly in August 1750, and his essential role in the Hunt became evident when it proved impossible to find a successor willing to devote the same amount of time and financial support. Quite quickly the Hunt was suspended and the hounds were transferred to other hunts. Fox Hall was closed and the hunting boxes were abandoned.

The third Duke (see XXII in colour section) endeavoured to restart the Hunt when he came of age, and, in fact, he was responsible for the magnificent stable block at Goodwood House and the new kennels (today housing the Goodwood Golf Club). In the intervening years, however, the hunting fraternity had discovered the attractions of the Shires, and the Hunt (now called the Duke of Richmond's Hunt) never, in fact, recovered its leading position. The kennels were finally closed in 1813.

LIGHT AND WATER: ROADS AND RUBBISH - The Council speaks.

The major events in the modern history of the village have been chronicled in the Minutes of the Parish Council. Boxgrove's council records begin in 1894, almost as soon as the first councils were formed. All parishes of more than 300 electors had to have a council, those with less than 100 had just a yearly meeting, for those between, a council was optional. The candidates were to be 'any adult, male or female, elector or non-elector who had been resident in the parish or within 3 miles of it for twelve months'. The population of Boxgrove in 1891 is given as 699. There is an interesting comparison with the figure for 1991 when the population was only 776. It should be noted that in 1891 all women were non-electors.

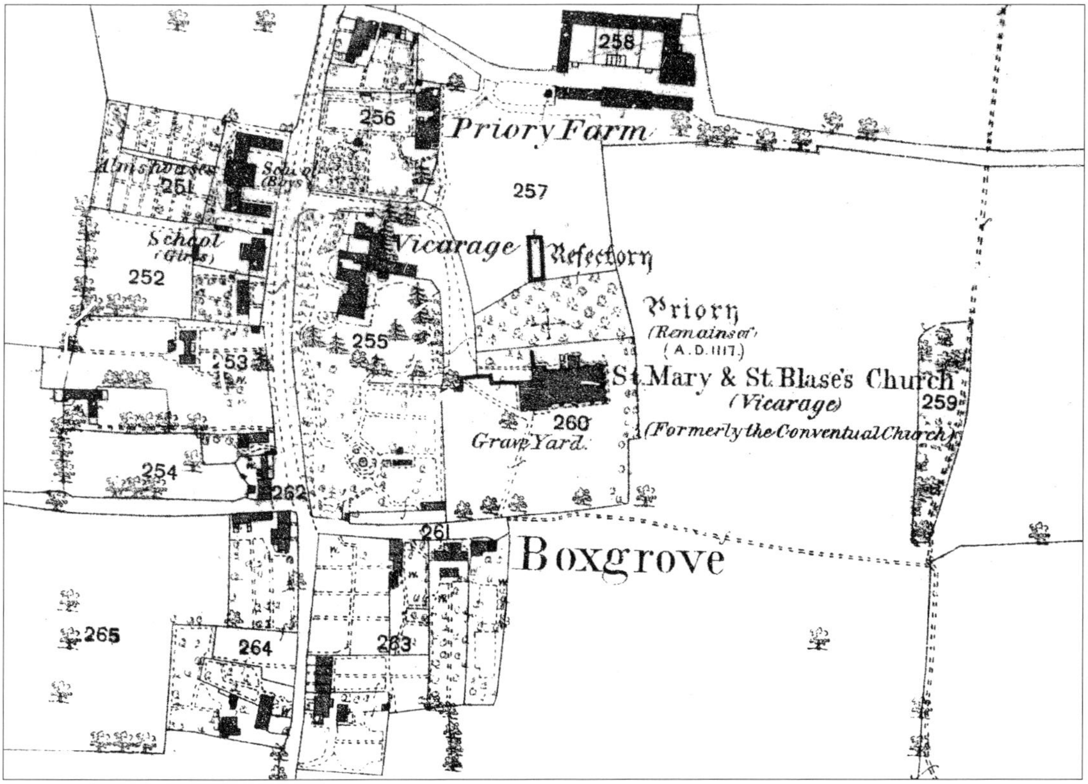

Figure 36. Boxgrove in 1875. As shown in the 1st Edition of the Ordnance Survey sheet LXII.1 (Goodwood Ms.E5051). Reproduced by courtesy of the Directors of the Goodwood Estate Company Limited with acknowledgements to the West Sussex Record Office and the County Archivist.

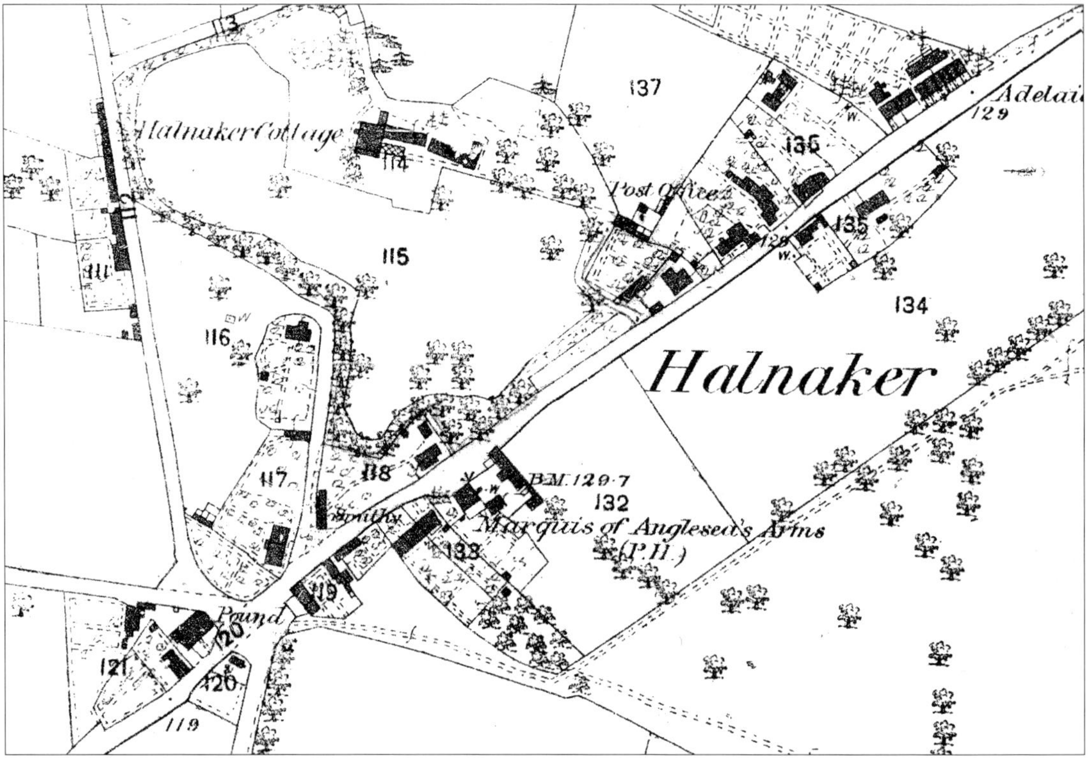

Figure 37. Halnaker in 1875. As shown in the 1st Edition of the Ordnance Survey sheet XLIX.13 (Goodwood Ms.E5051). Reproduced by courtesy of the Directors of the Goodwood Estate Company Limited with acknowledgements to the West Sussex Record Office and the County Archivist.

The members of the Council at the turn of the century (elected in 1899) were an interesting social mixture. The Chairman was Colonel Hillyard of Crocker Hill House, and the members included the Duke of Richmond, the Reverend Edward Hill (the vicar), Edward Atkey, Alexander Fogden and George Watkins (the three major farmers of Easthampnett, Strettington and Warehead), the Hon. Conynham Denison of Halnaker, and also Arthur Budd, the Crockerhill blacksmith, James Earwicker, the Halnaker carpenter and wheelwright and William Knight, the Boxgrove butcher. Successive vicars were members through to at least 1948 and the Duke of Richmond until 1928.

The main role of the council was to take over the non-ecclesiastical powers and duties of the parish vestry and churchwardens. These were, in the main, concerned with roads, poor relief and parish property. Parishes had been responsible for their roads since 1555 and many had appointed a highways surveyor. In 1862 local Justices of the Peace were given powers to form Highways Boards covering several parishes, and in 1888 County Councils became responsible for main roads and the District Councils for other roads in 1894; the Parish Councils were left to do the complaining. One of the first minutes of real business is in December 1913 when 'the Boxgrove Parish Council views with much concern and dissatisfaction the way in which the principal and much used roads are repaired'. The District Council replied that 'in view of the indefinite nature of the complaint, they were unable to take any action in the matter.' Boxgrove countered by suggesting some sites for repair and the use of 'granite or some similar material, to be coated with tar, this being especially required on account of the enormous traffic during the Goodwood Race week'.

Throughout the minutes, even up to the present day, there are complaints about the state of roads and paths in the care of the Rural District Council. For example, in 1920, the RDC was told that the road from Halnaker to Strettington was 'in a very dangerous state needing immediate attention'. This was in April. By the next council meeting in October, the Clerk was to 'ascertain what action had been taken as the Parish Council was of the opinion that nothing had been done up to the present time to remedy the complaint, although a large quantity of flints had been deposited by the side of the road for many months'. In addition, the local roadman had requested a wheelbarrow but had not received it and had had to borrow one from a friend.

In March 1936 a 30mph speed limit was requested in Boxgrove and Halnaker, but was only accepted by the County Council for Halnaker. The Council tried again in 1951. In 1935 the Council requested a 'Belisha Beacon' crossing (these had been introduced in 1934 along with 30 mph limits). It was to safeguard children from Tangmere crossing the A27. The request was turned down on the grounds that it would give the children 'an unwarranted sense of security'. In 1948 the Council members 'were of the unanimous opinion that a Round-a-bout (sic) was necessary at Halnaker Crossroads' (this was still being suggested in 1999). In May 1946 the Clerk was instructed to write to the Highways Department about 'the slippery and sloping surface of the road in Boxgrove Street on the east side near where the old pond used to be. Horses and pedestrians having fallen down in this particular place'.

The road system in the parish has seen several alterations over the years. It is the only transport available as the railway and canal are both to the south. The modern A27 Chichester to Arundel road is now the southern boundary of the civil parish, although the ecclesiastical parish extends much further. The road was made into a dual carriageway in 1977 and a new major junction with slip-

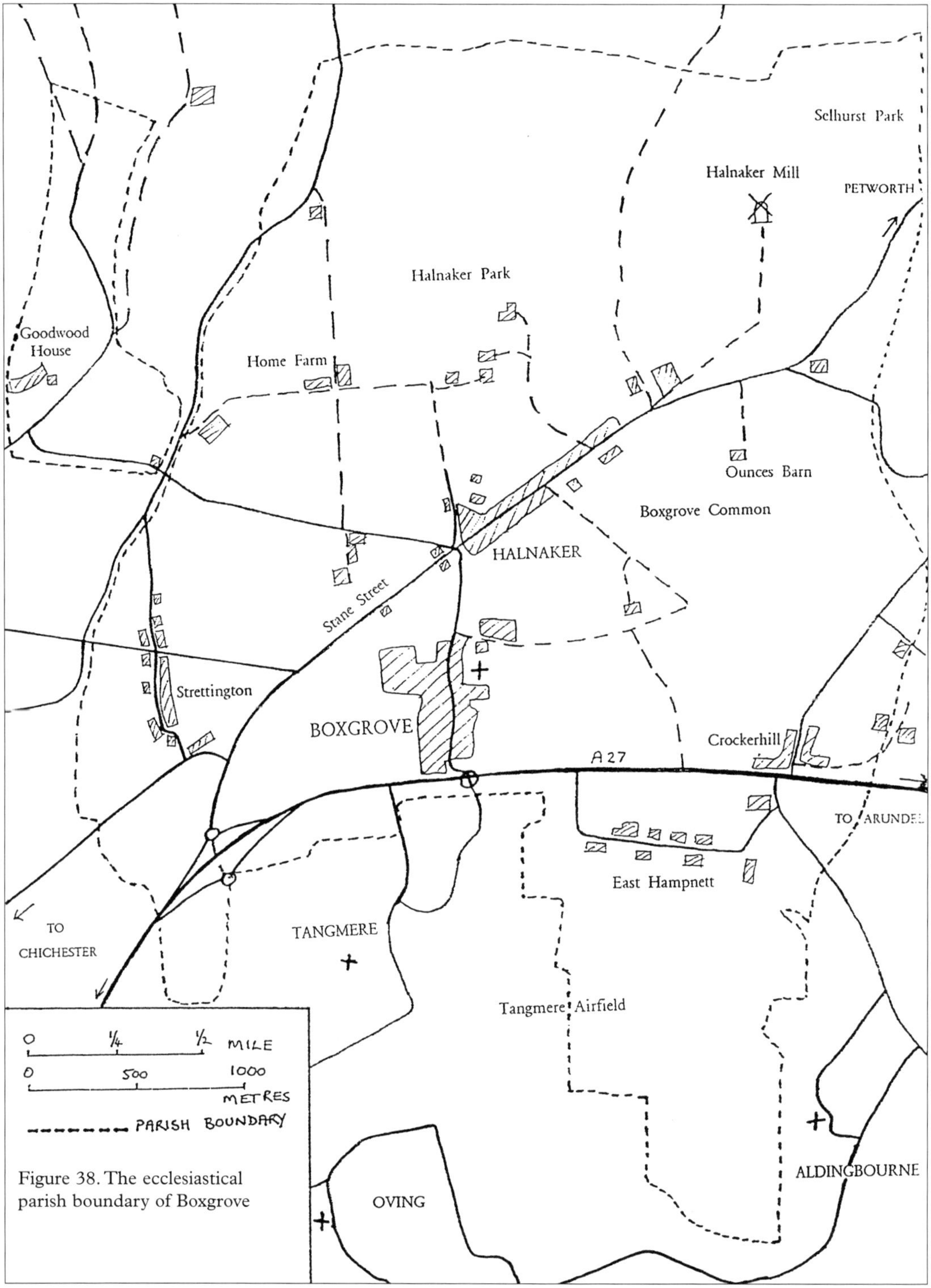

Figure 38. The ecclesiastical parish boundary of Boxgrove

roads and a flyover was provided at Temple Bar for the A285 Petworth road in 1992-3, just inside the south western corner of the parish. The Chichester to Petworth road is not in its 17th century position. The original route went through Goodwood Park (mainly outside Boxgrove Parish); there are still two milestones visible in the park. The second Duke of Richmond had this road blocked and re-routed through Halnaker on Stane Street. It is not clear why Stane Street had ceased to be used before this move. Boxgrove village itself, of course, is not on either main road, so has neither smithy nor public house, these being at Halnaker and Crockerhill, and their occupants in both places took an important part in village life.

Figure 39. Stane Street, c. 1925, the old Roman Road from Chichester to London, goes through the village. The Post Office, on the left, was demolished during the early 1950s. The postmaster during the early 1900s was Fred Gardner and letters arrived at 7am and 3pm. c. 1925.

Another recurrent theme was the disposal of rubbish. In 1929 the Council's attention had been drawn to 'house refuse and other rubbish deposited by the side of the road from Halnaker to Boxgrove Common (now Tinwood Lane). It was resolved that 'the Rural District Council be asked to erect a notice that rubbish, etc. must not be deposited there'. The reply, discussed the next month, was that the parish should provide a suitable dump from which the RDC would collect at periodic intervals. The Council 'unanimously resolved to recommend that 5 timber bins be provided, and the RDC to inform as to the cost'.By August the Parish Council had decided that they didn't need the bins as suitable dumps had been found. One of these was on the A27 Arundel Road 'opposite Mr. Cutler's garage' (now the filling station). In 1937 the RDC was asked to put up a notice board to warn users that the pit was for the ratepayers of Boxgrove only. But in June 1938 the RDC wrote announcing a fortnightly front door collection with a rate increase of 3.7d. The Parish Council accepted the decision but was of the opinion that much dissent would be created among many of the ratepayers at the increase. The collections began on 1 April 1939.

The two major developments in the village that caused much discussion were the water supply and the coming of electricity and street lighting. The water supply was first discussed in 1933, but by May of 1934 most wells, in spite of deepening, were dry, and the school had been without water 'for any purpose' for four months. A special Parish Meeting was held in June. The Council was proposing the motion that it urge the Rural District Council to negotiate at once with the Bognor Regis Urban District Council, to agree with the Chichester Corporation to supply water to the parishes of Boxgrove and Tangmere. The minutes record that 'After a long discussion in which many persons took part', an amendment was unanimously carried 'that in view of the serious shortage of water, the RDC be urged to take immediate steps to provide an adequate main supply'. However, in July there was a second meeting to consider the proposals sent by Bognor, at which these proposals were rejected on the grounds of excessive cost and inadequate service! The problem was that, while the parish was in the statutory area for Bognor to supply water, the Chichester pipes were in fact much nearer and would probably be cheaper. Bognor UDC was not prepared to relinquish its rights, and Chichester had sent a deputation to the Ministry of Health in London. The Ministry, however, could not help: an Act of Parliament would be needed, and even that would probably be opposed by Bognor. The scheme proposed would have cost £6,800 . It is not recorded who did supply the water in the end, but it would seem to have been Bognor as by 1935 there were fire hydrants along the line of the new water mains, and there are covers here and there with BRWC on them.

The possible supply of electricity is first mentioned in the 1935 minutes. The Clerk wrote 'It was reported to the meeting that there are several people desirous of having electric light if the supply could be extended to Halnaker'. The cost would be £400 to install plus a guarantee of £40 per annum. A circular letter was sent 'to all those who would be likely to take advantage of this service'. By July 1936 nine replies had been received and some new proposals were made: the Goodwood Estate was keen to have a supply to Warehead Farm, and the Rt. Hon. Reginald McKenna wanted a branch to a house to be built for him in Halnaker Park. They jointly would finance the supply.

Street lighting was first proposed for the village in December 1948. The Clerk minuted that 'there should be a standard electric light at the three places in the parish where the bus stops; it being so difficult to see after getting off a well lighted bus, and in the subsequent darkness an accident or personal injury might result'. Costings were obtained for a scheme of eleven columns for £300, with an annual cost of £4-10-0 per column. The parish would need to adopt the 1833 Lighting and Watching Act of Parliament. This was explained more fully at the parish council meeting in March of 1949. A loan could be raised at 3% interest. A special Parish Meeting was convened 'by Public Notices displayed at five different but conspicuous places in the Parish' for 11 March 1949; 26 people attended. The Act was adopted by the required two-thirds majority, then the lighting scheme was fully discussed. It was opposed by the vicar, the Reverend E. Popham, as an unnecessary expense benefitting such a small section of the community. The proposal to go ahead was finally passed by 15 votes to 6, but Mr. Popham stated that he would demand a poll on the question of the need for street lighting.

A second public meeting was held in July 1949, at which over sixty members of the parish were present. Considerable discussion took place, ending in a vote carried by a large majority. The motion stated: 'the time for carrying out this scheme is inopportune and it is therefore proposed that the minutes referring to the adoption of the Lighting and Watching Act at the previous meeting be annulled'. No further mention is made of this matter until the Annual Meeting in March 1962 when a question was asked. The Chairman said that the Parish Council would look into the matter but it was likely to be expensive. 'A year ago, 17 lamps would have cost £800 and a 3d rate for running costs. This without considering Halnaker, Crocker Hill and Strettington which would have to be included in any general lighting scheme.' The next year at the Parish AGM with some forty members of the public present, there was a long and detailed discussion of costs, increases to the rates and numbers of lamps. Halnaker and Strettington did not want any and, after a vote with a large majority against, the Chairman said that two years should elapse before a new vote. In fact it was not until August 1973 that a public meeting was called. At this it was decided not to provide any lighting immediately but to hold a referendum. The West Sussex County Council was now the street lighting authority and could be asked to supply some, but there was a long waiting period. A circular letter was sent out, and at a (new) meeting in January 1974 , with 62 of the parish present, the voting was 42 against, 18 for, and 2 not on the register. The proposal was therefore lost. The next discussion was five years later, when it was minuted that 'some form of street lighting seemed desirable, mainly in the interest of people without cars', and by May 1980 the Chairman reported that lighting had been provided in Boxgrove village at a cost of £5,554, for which a 6p rate was being raised. It had taken 32 years to be settled, and then only for part of the parish.

The question of accommodation and housing development was often discussed, but parish councils had, and still have, few powers in these matters, other than to make representations to higher authority. The first reference appears to be in 1914 when the Clerk was directed to reply to the RDC that 'the Parish Council considers that the number of houses for the working classes in Boxgrove is sufficient, and there is no necessity for providing additional housing accommodation.' However by December of 1918 the RDC were being asked to build 10 houses, three in Halnaker, four in Boxgrove and three in Strettington. By 1937 the Council considered 'the very serious shortage of houses' and recommended that the RDC build 12 cottages in Boxgrove.

After the Second World War the minutes include a detailed list of 13 cottages deemed too expensive to be made fit for habitation, many damaged by enemy action; a list of 18 that could be improved and 'three further needed to accommodate persons displaced'. In 1946 the RDC was being asked to complete the scheme of 'the Housing Estate' by the erection of the eight houses 'so urgently needed'.

Since the building of the council houses in Crouch Cross Lane there have been many more houses erected, the main groups being the sixteen houses and bungalows at the south end of Boxgrove called Priory Close, in 1965, and the more recent development on the Boxgrove Farm site, now named Prior's Acre, completed in 1997, with 18 flats in an enlarged main house, and about forty new houses and bungalows. A few houses have been built infilling gaps in The Street, with one site converted from an enlarged bungalow (originally built in 1927 for the chauffeur of the then owner of the farm) to a terrace of five houses. Full details of the development of the housing would take a whole chapter and much more research than time currently allows. The Parish Council is still empowered to consider all planning applications in its area, and can make recommendation thereon to the District planning authority.

The other major discussions in the Council from the 1950s onwards have been on the development of the Village Hall and the Playing Field, and the leasing of the Hall to the Village Club. The Club is now no longer in operation and all the buildings are back in the care of the Council. There have been some developments in the other hamlets of the parish, but they do not feature largely in the Council minutes. Part of the farm buildings at Strettington have been converted into small business units. An official Caravan Park for travellers has been established in Easthampnett . A poultry processing plant in Halnaker was built in the 1970s and extended in the 1980s. In the same period buildings at

Priory Farm were converted to small industrial units and now house companies employing about twenty people. Individual houses have been inserted into all the old residential areas and the farming is now almost entirely commercial lettuce growing, with wheat every three years in rotation, and the land of Boxgrove Farm to the west of the village is now mainly horse paddocks. The gravel workings on Boxgrove Common where Boxgrove Man was found have been worked beyond commercial viability and are now deserted.

MEMORIES OF VILLAGE LIFE IN BOXGROVE AND HALNAKER

We have now reached a period within range of living memory and in 1988 Mrs Austen-Ward, on behalf of the Boxgrove Women's Institute conducted a number of tape recorded interviews with older residents of the village.

These recollections give a first hand insight into life in this area from the late ninteenth century.

The earliest memories recorded are about the life of Amos Hall as told by his wife, Maggie.

Amos was born in 1877 and died in 1966. His family lived in Eartham where his father was an agricultural labourer for Sir William Bird. Sir William lived in what is now Great Ballards School.

'Amos was nine when he started work. He was rook scaring on Sir William's land.....he had two fields to keep them off. Somehow or other - I don't know how he got his fire - he used to bake a swede in the ashes: a swede what he'd pulled up from the field. He'd bake it and have that for his dinner.'

There were sixteen children in Amos' family. At some point in his childhood there was an outbreak of diphtheria in Eartham and four of the children in his family died in three weeks.

'Of course, they took them to the fever hospital. But when Amos fell ill she (the mother) wouldn't let them take him: he evidently only had it mild.'

When Amos was sixteen his father died. There were still four young children at home, so Amos worked to keep his mother and the family until his mother remarried. It was remarked that his mother married the lodger and, indeed, it was very common for village families to have a lodger in spite of the smallness of the cottages and the large size of families. There were a lot of single men working as agricultural labourers during the 1880's, and right through into the Twenties.

Maggie Hall, herself, was born in 1894 at Stedham, near Midhurst. Her father was a shepherd. He was paid sixteen shillings a week and had a tied cottage. The labourers on the farm could help themselves to vegetables from the farm ground.

'In our schooldays we often had vegetables and gravy for dinner. Sunday dinner used to be stewed rabbit because Dad was allowed to carry a gun and set wires. All the men had their set parts to set wires for rabbits. I don't think we got much meat during the week.'

Maggie was expected to help at home, and one of her jobs was to turn the grinder to cut the swedes for the sheep to eat, a job she returned to decades later when she helped Amos in the fields at Goodwood. As a child she had few toys, and she remembers how the girls made dolls by wrapping a rag round a bundle of twigs. Children then 'made their own fun as best they could.'

Many families in Boxgrove have been 'local' for generations, including that of two sisters, now Mrs Goble and Mrs Patten. They were born at Rose Cottage, Halnaker - it was two cottages then. There were ten in the family, three boys and seven girls and they all slept in the same room in three beds. There was one other bedroom. Downstairs there was a scullery, kitchen and parlour. The parlour was 'kept for best'. The privy was down the bottom of the garden. This consisted of a shed with two seats inside, one large and one small! Underneath the seats were a couple of buckets. Needless to say there was no water on tap, no sanitation, and no electricity or gas. This description is very typical of rural cottages, and many were not modernised until well into the Fifties and early Sixties.

Rose cottage was rented from the farmer who worked Halnaker Mill. It had a long garden in which the sisters' father grew fruit and vegetables and kept chickens. Most gardens in rural areas were used for this purpose. The garden provided an important supplement to the family income. But poverty was not a problem - 'If we were poor we weren't aware of it.' The father of the two girls was never out of work. 'We ate good plain food, cooked on an open fire, with all the vegetables cooked in one pot.' The only meat they had was rabbit which their father caught. Otherwise they were sent down to the butcher's in Boxgrove for bones to make soup. The butcher's shop was at the entrance to Priory Farm, in what is now Priory Cottage. If their mother made pies or cakes they were baked in the Baker's oven. She never went shopping. A number of Chichester shops sent round a horse and cart to deliver groceries, or she could ask the carrier, Mr McCarthy, to bring back what was required. McCarthy was apparently quite a character, and was known as 'Cabby'. 'Football, horse racing and home-made wine were his strong points', recalls Jim Clarke.

As children the two sisters went gleaning in the fields for corn to feed the chickens. During the First World War their mother helped with the harvest in the fields at Westhampnett. She collected the wheat into stooks and stacked them, and the girls would help her.

Discipline did not seem particularly strict, although they were not expected to answer back, or to 'be familiar' with grown-ups. At table they sat in silence. On Sunday afternoon their father gave each of his children a farthing to spend at the sweet shop at Halnaker. Sometimes the family would go up into Goodwood Park and play rounders, or they would play in the woods. But they were never allowed out to play in the evenings!

Figure 40. The village shop at Halnaker, on the right, belonging to F. Pennicott whose family also ran the Singleton shop. The thatched cottage was badly damaged by fire during the 1930s and later demolished. Blunden's fuel yard and the village bakery, both just out of the picture, were sited at the crossroads.

Church dominated Sundays. They went to service in the morning and evening and also attended Sunday School. While they were still at school '..... the vicar, the Reverend Hill, died and all the children had to walk past his coffin to look at the body and pay their last respects.' Respect of a different sort was also paid to the Gordon-Lennoxes. They had to curtsey to all the family and also the vicar and his wife. But they were not expected to curtsey to Lady Palliser who lived locally. Such were the conventions of their day.

Neither sister liked school especially. They attended Boxgrove school when they were five until they were fourteen years old. Their teacher was a Miss Brown. She was very strict and they did not dare speak. However there were two 'treats' a year for the village children. At Christmas, the Duke and Duchess of

Richmond provided a tree, and a little present for each child. They sang songs and were given a silver sixpence (which was taken home to mother, of course). In the summer the children all had a trip to the beach at Bognor in the carrier's horse and cart. When the weather was fine they were allowed to play in the lanes - there was little, if any, traffic then, and the roads were rough cobbles or dirt tracks.

Both of the sisters went into service when they left school - they never considered doing anything else, as most village girls did the same. Mrs Goble started work as a between-maid at Lavant House. She was paid ten shillings (50p) a month, and her keep, and she believes she had to buy her own uniform. She started her daily chores at 6.30 am and was on duty until 9.00 or 10.00 at night. During the morning, once the family were up, she helped the upstairs maid clean the bedrooms and in the afternoon she helped in the kitchen. Once a fortnight the cooking range had to be cleaned down and the flues scraped - a horrible job! After four years Mrs Goble went to work for Lord and Lady March at Molecomb. She was 'much happier at Molecomb'. 'I remember each servant had their own ration of jam, butter and sugar, and this was put on a plate with their name. All the children were polite to the servants'. Mrs Patten joined her sister at Molecomb for a time, and the two girls would save up their sugar to take home to mother. Most of their wages went to mother as well. Of course, it must be remembered that female servants were generally young, single women, as were the two sisters at this time.

Later, Mrs Patten went to work for Sir William Bird at Eartham. Sir William and his wife had no children. Perhaps partly to compensate for this they lavished a great deal of care and affection on their servants and estate workers. They were a much loved couple. There were nine servants in the house - three house maids, three kitchen maids, a butler, a footman and a trainee.

The estate was a large one and produced most of its own food - milk, butter, flour, fruit, vegetables, chickens, partridge, and pheasant etc. It is interesting to note just how self sufficient a large estate could be at that time.

During the First World War Sir William and his wife made sure that the poor did not suffer and provided them with blankets and shoes. When he died he left a small legacy to each of his workmen.

Another Halnaker family were the Parkers. Harry Parker was born at about the same time as Mrs Goble, and lived just across the road from her at the pub known then, as now, as the Anglesey Arms. Harry is, alas, now dead but he was a great character and had many tales to tell of what went on and who lived where

Figure 41. A loaded wagon of bavins outside the Anglesey Arms. The bavins were probably being delivered to Blunden's, the village fuel merchants. The empty wagon appears to be on its way to collect a similar load, and the two drivers have obviously stopped for refreshment.

and what they did.

People seemed to have a great deal of fun at the pub. Most of those who frequented it were 'locals'. Not many 'new' people came by. There was a room at the back of the pub where the Fathers' and Mothers' Guild met. This room had a brick floor, and Harry had vivid recollections of the women dancing so much that they kicked up the brick dust which swirled about their crinolines. In those days there was only one bar, no 'posh bar'. Beer was 2d a pint and bread and cheese with a few pickled onions was also 2d. There would often be sing-songs to the accompaniment of an accordion and tambourine. At lunch time the men would play quoits in the field next to the pub. They had steel or iron quoits that they had to pitch over a steel spike.

There were a lot of farm buildings around the pub then - stables and cow sheds. The family kept cows and sold milk and butter. Naturally there was a large vegetable garden, and chickens and pigs were kept. After Harry's father died in 1916 his mother ran the pub with the help of Harry and his brother Fred.

Harry could recall a number of 'village characters' from his childhood days. A blind man lived in one of the cottages in front of Boxgrove Stores, and to earn a living he made baskets from rushes and wicker, the sort with two straps that workmen wore over their shoulders. There were tales also of a village witch, some poor old soul who scared the children. At Boxgrove corner Old Ned Smith lived in a thatched cottage. 'When I was a nipper he had a housekeeper called Mrs Hyde - used to bring up a pig on a string and get a pint of porter for 4d.' At one time there was a lodger in the same cottage who was 'kind to tramps'. He used to hide pipes and tobacco in a hole in the wall for the tramps to collect when passing by. Yes, Harry had a great fund of stories to recount.

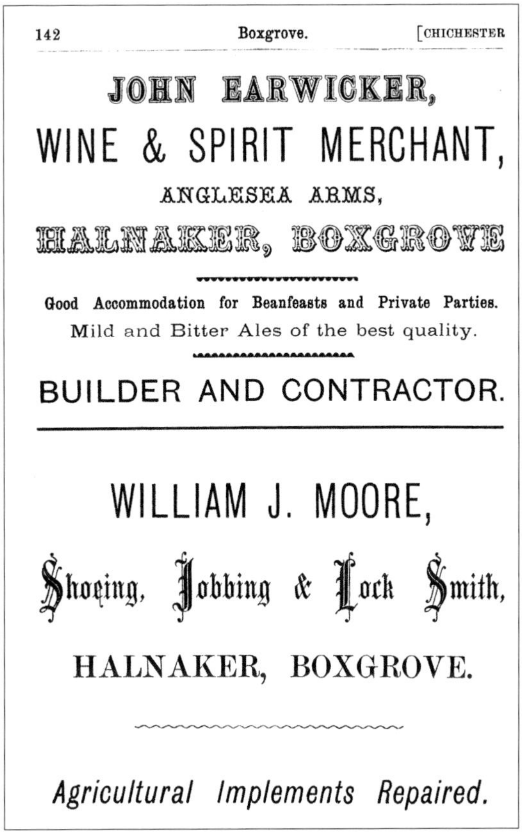

Figure 42. Advertisements from 'The Sussex Directory' of 1886 for services available in Halnaker.

In 1910 many services were available from local tradesmen. Mr Jim Clarke recalls the wide range on offer by people who were all residents either in Boxgrove or Halnaker. There was a blacksmith, carrier, postman, taxi service, butcher's shop, general store, a gent's hairdresser, boot and shoe repairer, milkman, wheelwright and carpenter, baker, miller, policeman and undertaker.

During the Twenties and Thirties life seems to have carried on much as before. The Depression and its accompanying unemployment does not appear to have had much effect on Boxgrove and the surrounding area. Families were smaller with, perhaps, a slightly higher standard of living but, by and large, the way of life was very similar to that of previous decades.

Mrs Jellet came to Chichester from Norfolk during the First World War. She married a local man and moved to Strettington in the early Twenties. 'Our income then was about twenty five shillings a week, plus a war pension of twelve shillings. We paid 12/6d a month rent with rates on top. Out of that I had to pay everything for my babies. We had two boys- the first one was 9lb and the second 9$^1/_2$lb. You had to pay the nurse and you had to buy everything that was required for the confinement. If you booked a doctor you had to pay £3 whether he came or not. So I didn't book a doctor.

'We grew all our own vegetables. I did my shopping in Chichester. I walked in and carried it back, and I took the children: well it was easier carrying the shopping with a pram.

'We lived in a little cottage at Strettington, up towards Waterbeach. We lived in the centre one and had two bedrooms, sitting room and kitchen. We shared the wash-house with the other neighbours. We had well water and oil lamps and just a bucket for a toilet.

'People couldn't smoke or drink much then. After I had the two children my husband only earned thirty shillings a week; they took his war pension away.... He had two shillings to pay for his tobacco and 6d of that he saved in the Slate Club in case he was ill. I made my own wine, bottled fruit and jam. I belonged to the Mothers' Union and we paid into that for clothing etc. We bought second-hand clothes sometimes and there were jumble sales. I made my own clothes and clothes for the boys, as I had a treadle machine given me. My husband used to wear out the knees of his trousers because he did manual work. And out of the parts that weren't worn I used to get a little suit or trousers for the boys.

'I paid into a Christmas Club, and I saved in the Halfpenny Club. It came to about thirty shillings - that was a fortune. I did all my Christmas shopping out of that. We made all our own decorations - paper chains and such like. They don't seem to use these today. I'd save up all the little bits of silver paper....we made our own Christmas.

'They (the boys) only had one good present, and they'd have an apple, an orange and sweet nick-nacks. We did eventually get a second-hand gramophone with a trumpet and a few records.

'The children used to go to Sunday School, and I always went to church every Sunday. I belonged to the Mothers' Union; it was very religious. We used to have a talk from the vicar in the church. Then we went into the vicarage and had our tea, and the vicar's wife, Mrs Popham, talked to us. She'd often get a speaker. The talks were always about the Bible and leading a good life. We always said grace before and after meals, and we always said prayers with the children when they went to bed. My husband came to church on Sunday evening, and every so often he would come to Communion, but not regular. We always went to church twice on Sunday, and later the children were in the choir, and they were servers as well.'

Someone else who remembers this period is Mrs Deadman. Her parents came

Figure 43. Mr Sawyer, the village blacksmith and farrier, stands outside the forge at Halnaker. It is still in use today.

from Devon originally, but she was born and brought up in Halnaker in Forge Cottage. Her father was the village blacksmith - shoeing horses, mending cartwheels and doing other iron work repairs. There were many more horses at this time as horses were used to draw ploughs, haul logs, pull carts and drays - few tradesmen had motor vans. Her father used special coal and pumped the bellows. He employed only one other man.

The family income was about average for country folk, and it was supplemented, needless to say, with fruit and vegetables from the garden. They kept hens and cockerels as well. Mrs Deadman and her sisters attended Boxgrove school. She liked school and remembers Empire Day when the children saluted the flag. When she left school at fourteen she went into service - 'most girls went into service.' As has been remarked before, not a lot had changed since before the Great War. Mrs Deadman's first job was at Fontwell where she was the under housemaid - one of five servants. She worked from 6.30 am to bedtime (10.00 pm), laying fires, cleaning, sweeping etc. She lived in and was paid sixty-five pounds a year and allowed half a day off a week with half a day every other Sunday. She spent ten years in service before getting married to a plumber who worked on the Goodwood estate. Their first home was one of three cottages that used to be on the corner of The Street and Crouch Cross

Figure 44. The former vicarage at Boxgrove, its stonework masked by ivy, c. 1900. The vicarage used to be where Priory Gate House now stands and was demolished in the late 1930s. Presumably the man with the dogs is the vicar himself!

Lane. These cottages were severely damaged during the Second World War and had to be pulled down.

An interesting account of life in Boxgrove just after the First World War has been provided by Mrs Farmer, the elder child of Richard Wells, vicar of Boxgrove from 1911 to 1926, and his wife Katherine. She was born at Boxgrove vicarage on 4 July 1913 and was christened Mary Katherine by her father on 6 August. Her father was thirty nine and her mother thirty five, and her brother Richard was born three years later. She recalls

'Our vicarage was a pleasant brick and flint built house with the main windows facing south and east over the large garden. At the back were the stables, coach house, harness room, apple house, pig sty and other outbuildings. Indoors, downstairs was the hall, dining room, study, drawing room, servants hall, pantry, kitchen etc., and on the first floor the nursery, four bedrooms and two dressing rooms, a boxroom and bathroom, with three or four servants bedrooms on the top floor.

'The household consisted of our nurse, housemaid, parlourmaid and cook with a daily gardener and garden boy. Each had their well defined daily work.

The cook would rise at 6.30 am and the other maids a little later. She would light the kitchen range. The housemaid would do the fires and the parlourmaid bring my parents early morning tea, and lay the breakfast. She would also bring up cans of hot water and place them, covered by a towel, in the bedroom washbasins. Breakfast was at 8.30 and my father would say Matins at the church at 9.15. My mother and I would accompany him and say the responses sometimes. My mother would then have her daily discussion with the cook to plan the meals. On Mondays the laundry was sorted and packed in a huge wicker hamper and wheeled to a special flat barrow by Arthur Salisbury, the gardener, across the 'wobble gates' to Mrs Hammond, who did our washing. Meanwhile the lamps were cleaned and the wicks trimmed on the 'slab' inside the side door and the knives cleaned and sharpened by the garden boy who had already polished the shoes in a shed across the backyard. The house was swept and polished, the living rooms before breakfast and the bedrooms and upstairs landing later. After lunch at 1.00 pm the maids changed into their afternoon dresses. These were black with frilly cap and apron, morning dresses being blue cotton with plain cap and apron. In the morning we did lessons in the dining room with Miss Willard, our governess, who bicycled over from Tangmere. She never removed her hat and veil and wore a high necked collar. Our favourite lesson was drawing at which she excelled. We learnt a long list of spelling words each day. My father always wrote the next Sunday's sermon on Monday morning, revised it later in the week and learnt it on Saturday evening. He was a good gardener and handyman and had a carpenter's shop at the bottom of the garden. The vicarage had to be painted every five years outside and he did most of this himself. Every afternoon he would mount his bicycle and go visiting. Sometimes I would sit in front on a hard metal carrier and accompany him. He called all the men by their Christian names and took a great interest in their work and gardens and said he was more often called upon to heal a sick pig than their souls! We did not have a car but my mother had a pony and cart and later gave us a donkey and a smart brown and yellow cart (which she bought in Portsmouth and drove back herself). We drove out on most afternoons; Mabel Longland, our nanny, driving and often one of the maids coming too. On Fridays in the winter we drove to Lavant House for a dancing class. It was often very cold and we had a tin, carpet- covered carriage hot water bottle for our feet. Later we had bicycles.

'We had no telephone and urgent news had to be telegraphed. There was a sense of excitement and dread when the telegraph boy, with his red bike and pill

Figure 45.Halnaker crossroads in 1910 with a group of well dressed youngsters.

box hat, was seen at the door with an orange coloured envelope. If we wanted to use the telephone we would go up to the post office, run by Ena Gardner at Halnaker.

'Our milk would be delivered by Mr King with his float drawn by the old white pony from Mr Watkins' farm at Warehead. Bread and groceries would be brought from Mrs Wheatley's at Halnaker cross-roads. Mr Henly was the baker and we never knew whether his white face was caused by the hot atmosphere or if it was covered with flour. We would go up to Mrs Wheatley's with our Saturday pennies to buy sweets from the big jars and come away with them done up in a twist of blue paper. Meat was delivered from Chichester, and we fetched two pounds of butter every week from the Goodwood Dairy where we were welcomed by rosy cheeked Miss Miller, the dairymaid, and taken into the large, cool dairy to see the collection of china animals and birds on the marble shelves where great pans of milk stood.

'My father and mother were involved in all the village activities. Father was Rural Dean and a member of the Rural District Council. My mother was Enrolling Member of the Mothers' Union and had a flourishing Girls' Friendly Society, who met in the vicarage garden in the summer. She helped start the Boxgrove Women's Institute about 1920. She was always full of fun

Figure 46. Children playing what appears to be a game of marbles in the main street of Boxgrove, c. 1910. The entrance to Church Lane is just visible in the foreground on the right.

and much loved.

'In the summer we played tennis and croquet and clock golf on the vicarage lawn, mown by our old pony with leather boots over his iron shoes. We had home-made stilts and bows and arrows and our own house in the garden built by my father. I had a wooden hoop and was rather envious of the iron ones controlled with an iron hook which the village boys propelled down the dusty road outside the school. Conkers, marbles and hopscotch followed each other with the seasons.

'One of my first memories was Armistice Day, 11 November 1918, a rather gloomy, misty day, but we walked up to Halnaker with the push chair waving flags and shouting "The War's gone over" and it seemed as if a great weight had lifted from all the grown-ups. Flags were poking out of cottage windows and everyone seemed happy. The next summer there was a celebration party in Goodwood Park for all the children. We drove up from Boxgrove in a farm wagon, ran races, and had a lovely tea and were each presented with a medal on a red, white and blue ribbon. Every Empire Day, 24 May, there was a special ceremony round the flag staff in front of the boys' school in the centre of the almshouses, and we were addressed by some elderly colonel or some other pillar of the Empire.

'Ash Wednesday was an occasion when all the school children marched to church. Easter and Harvest Festival we loved because it meant decorating the church with flowers and fruit and vegetables. On Sunday mornings the Duke and Mr Watkins, the two churchwardens, would arrive for morning service in bowler hats and we would pick a buttonhole for each of them and shyly present it. Matins was attended by all the local 'gentry' but I enjoyed evensong most when the church was filled with villagers and the singing was loud and hearty. In winter the lamps were turned out, one by one, after the service by Fred Budd and Arthur Salisbury, the sidesmen. I can still smell the smoke and feel the eerie darkness as we trooped out of the church and across the moonlit garden.

'On our birthdays in July we went in George Bowles' village taxi to Bognor, having prayed fervently for a fine day. If wet you had to make your castles under the pier.

Figure 47. A charabanc typical of those operating in Sussex around 1922.

'Another exciting treat was the annual Women's Institute outing. We boarded the green Southdown charabanc outside the almshouses. Each row of seats had a door at either end and they rose in tiers towards the back. The huge hood was folded down and we had a wonderful view as we whirled through the summer air with hay and bean fields smelling sweetly on either side. We would pick up outlying people as we headed for Brighton or Worthing or Littlehampton. Mrs Dykes, at her little cottage in Aldingbourne, always wore a wide brimmed black hat with a wreath of different garden flowers around it, sweet peas one year, roses another.

Figure 48. Racing at Goodwood in July 1929 viewed from the Trundle. The finish of the West Dean Selling Plate won by Mr. R. C. Daws' 'Quick Light' (Bartham up). Reproduced by courtesy of the Trustees of the Goodwood Collection.

'The event of the year was, of course, Race Week beginning then, as now, on the last Tuesday in July. For this my father, together with most other occupants of sizeable houses, always tried to 'Let for Goodwood'. The same London racegoers took ours every year and we would pack up large trunks and even a tin bath with a lid and go off by train to our grandparents.

'One of the last exciting times I remember at Boxgrove was the General Strike in May 1926. I think the only wireless set in the village was owned by the Eames family at Priory Farm. We would gather round and take down the news which we would then pin up on the village noticeboard outside Mrs Hewson's at the club. My brother had recently started school as a boarder at Sunningdale and was delighted that there was no train running to take him back after the Easter holidays. I remember his fury when Lady March kindly offered her car with Charlie Tilbury, the chauffeur, to drive him back.

'I must mention some of the village characters who lived and worked in Boxgrove in those days. The almshouse ladies were our near neighbours and

Figure 49. Celebrating a win! Goodwood races July 1929. Reproduced by courtesy of the Trustees of the Goodwood Collection.

visited most days: Mrs Peachey, who lived to be a hundred, Miss Clemens, Mrs Shippam, Miss Goff, and Miss Earwicker were some of them. Nurse Hind, our district nurse, was a friend in need to many, travelling round her large district on her bicycle with her black Gladstone bag in all weathers. Mr Hewson was the village barber. My brother did not like going to him and complained that he pulled his hair. Kitty Hewson, his daughter, was a good pianist and played for village dances. Tom Earwicker was the carpenter. His shop was surrounded by wooden well-heads which we would climb up onto and pretend we were on horseback. Bee Earwicker, his daughter, was very smart as she was a sales lady at Bourne and Hollingsworth in London. Mr McCarthy was the carrier and he and his wife would sit up in front of the covered van stopping to pick up orders on their way to Chichester and delivering them in the evening, with news from the outside world. On Boat Race day we would lie in bed eagerly awaiting the sound of clip clopping coming up the road and our nanny would come and tell us if Oxford had won before we could go to sleep. Mr Long was head keeper and Ted Glasspool the under keeper. Father would shoot at Goodwood in the autumn and winter and bring back pheasants for the pot and blue jay's feathers for my black felt hat. Mr Brock was head gardener at Goodwood. The annual flower show was held in the old Real Tennis Court at the bottom of Goodwood kitchen garden. Most of the village men worked on the local farms; Mr Brown, the large Scots farmer at Home Farm, Mr Reddaway at Strettington, Mr Whittle and then Mr Eames at Priory Farm, Mr Taylor at East Hampnett. All of these I remember together with many more who made up our little world: Mr Blunden the coal merchant, Mr and Mrs Parker (very grand) of the Anglesey Arms, The Luffs, Glasspools, Tapners, Gardners, Emersons, who walked three miles from Molecomb to school every day wet or shine, Budds, Greens, Pages, Hammonds, Houghtons, Phillips, Symes, Terrys, Hunts, Burns, Whites, Lowdons, Suttons, Norrells, Irelands, Aldreds, Earwickers and not forgetting the three Miss Palmers, who were very prim.'

Village life during the Thirties is recalled by Marmie Pitman. Marmie's family were local people on both his mother's and father's side. He himself was born in what is now a restaurant on the A27. Back in the Twenties it was a Goodwood house.

'My father worked on the Goodwood Estate and then he worked for the Council looking after the village - clearing the ditches and looking after the verges and hedges, that sort of thing. We moved from that house on the Arundel Road into where my granny lived. (Marmie's granny lived in one of the flint cottages opposite Boxgrove Stores, the one that is on the end next to Church Lane.) That house was in our family over a hundred and fifty years. My mother's parents worked for Goodwood. My grandfather was the sexton for the church. He done fifty years at the church, and his wife, my granny, done twenty five years - cleaning the church.'

Marmie can remember clearly what the village was like in the Thirties. 'Along by the flint wall, where I used to live, and up Church Lane, that used to be six pieces of allotment...I remember when I was going to school, just round in Church Lane, they dug a new well because of the drought. Before they done that Goodwood used to bring a big tank down on a horse-drawn cart, and round into Church Lane for the villagers, because of the drought. So, they sank this new

Figure 50. The view looking south along Boxgrove's main street, 1950s. The Boxgrove Stores/Post Office, on the right is still doing good business forty years later.

well, where the white house is on the corner, by what was then the allotments. There was a gate into the well, and it was fenced off. Anyone could use the well. The men used to walk up with a yoke on their shoulders, with pails. They did that when they came home from work. They'd draw their water, and that had to last them until the next night. There was no sinks or bathrooms then. We didn't have one put in that house until 1960.

'I can remember when Blunden's used to bring the coal down on a solid tyre lorry. I was about eight. Coal was 1.11d a hundredweight then. But people was only getting a pound or two a week, so we didn't buy much coal. We went out wooding.

'Now each of those houses where we lived had a big copper in the shed. We heated the water with wood. Blunden's had horses and carts go up into the wood and, you know the young chestnut trees? They would buy the rights to clear one part of the wood - an acre or two acres. They used to chop them all down and make the fencing stakes, hurdles and what have you. Then all the rough stuff they would bundle up into what they call faggots. You used to buy them for, say, 3d or 4d each. They used to be about four feet long and they'd poke them up underneath the copper.

'When we were children we used to go up with the men into the woods and have a ride on a cart. We used to go right up to Benges, along past Stud Farm. Then we used to have to walk home. They'd put the bundles like stacks of corn on the cart and trundle it home. That was in the morning, then we'd go up again in the afternoon.

'The baker used to come round every day with a basket on his arm. They were the old cottage loaves - a top and a bottom. The milkman used to come from Warehead Farm up in Halnaker. They had a little pony and cart and a big milk churn in the back with a tap on it. An old boy up in Halnaker, he used to come round and turn the tap and fill his can up. He had a little ladle with a long arm, and he used to pour the milk out as you wanted it, at the door.

'The old boy that kept the shop, well, he had pig sties up behind there and he had hens and ducks running around. Me and my brother used to go round finding the eggs in the hedgerows and we used to take them into the shop. He gave us sweets for that, because we didn't have any money to spend on sweets. I used to get a bar of toffee - a foot long, an inch wide and half an inch thick.

'Everybody had to walk in my grandad's day. He used to walk from Lavant into Chichester, get his pension, do a bit of shopping and then walk back. I've known him do that in his seventies and eighties . . . There was an old boy used to live over at Valdoe. He used to be bent right over and walk with a stick. He worked on the farm and they had fields all over. He'd walk to wherever they were threshing - right down to Wittering or Selsey, and then he'd walk all the way home after he had done his day's work. They used to put the sheaves of corn up in the fields, and they used horses to pull the binders and cut the corn and throw the sheaves out. The men would come along and stand the sheaves up, about six or eight in a stook, and then they'd put them in a rick. They used to thatch the rick to stop the water getting in. A thatcher would do that job. In the winter they used to thresh it out with a steam engine driving the drum.

'I didn't mind school, but I was glad to leave. We used to have to go up to Halnaker Park for football. We used to march up with the schoolmaster walking behind with his cane. If we had Sports Day we would do it all up there. And the men used to play football. During the Second World War the Duke of Richmond took the football pitch up and ploughed it up for the war effort. That's how we come to have this bit of land down here, in the village. They gave it to the village provided we fenced it.

'When we was at school we used to go out for nature walks. We used to have students come out each summer, one to each class. That was all right, we used to get on all right with them. They took us out all round the woods, then we'd have to come back and draw certain leaves and patterns.

'They used to have Empire Day. There would be a flagpole in the middle of the almshouses lawn. They raised the flag and we had to go outside and sing "Raise the Flag on High", and go to church - then we'd have a half day holiday, so that was all right that was.

'You went to school when you was five until you was fourteen. We were split according to age. This brick one (the school) is the new school. There was a wooden school and then it burnt down while we were on summer holiday. Mr Mason (the headmaster) used to put us older boys to work in the garden - dig his garden and look after his greenhouse. That's how I went gardening when I left. I worked over in the big house near the church with Mr Salisbury. He looked after the churchyard as well and I worked with him.

'The Tipteers were good. They did like a play and sang songs. We used to go up the (village) hall and we used to have a good evening's entertainment.'

The Tipteers were active before the First World War and then they faded out until the early thirties when they were revived by Mr Sharp from Fishbourne. They performed a mummers' play loosely based on the story of the Crusades. During the winter the Tipteers performed at Goodwood House and most large houses and hotels in the district. They even performed at the Albert Hall on one occasion!

The Women's Institute, together with the Mothers' Union provided the main opportunities for social contact for women in the village between the wars.

Mrs Jellet was a fund of knowledge about the Women's Institute. In those early days it was always run by someone who was 'somebody'. Past Presidents include Hilda, Duchess of Richmond.

'All Goodwood people were expected to join, just the same as they were expected to go to church. Westhampnett people came, and Tangmere - they all belonged. There was a good social mix and we had a hundred and more members'.

The Boxgrove Women's Institute then held it's meetings in the afternoons. The women generally walked there, of course, and took their children with them. The children were often asleep and would be put in the hall. The meetings were not dissimilar to those of today, although there was more emphasis on the home and domestic crafts.

The Second World War, inevitably, saw many changes take place in people's lives, and the work done by Women's Instutute members during this period reveals so clearly the many ways in which everyone was affected by the war effort. To quote Mrs Jellett again:

'We (the Women's Instutute) did a lot during the war. They had troops up at Goodwood House. The Women's Institute members used to go up there mending - you know, socks and that. One Friday we went up and we didn't have to do a lot of needlework but we had to pack a lot of bags. There was first aid, soap and flannel. We didn't know what we were doing it for. But in a few days we heard they'd opened the Second Front - D Day. So I always felt the Women's Institute took a little part in that.'

The Woman's Institute also started jam-making and bottling in the village hall - plums, tomatoes, blackberries and so on. The members bought their own canning equipment. Boxes of vegetables were bought from a man who used to come round, or they would buy from local people, and the filled cans and bottles were collected for distribution.

The Women's Institute ladies ran a number of schemes in the village during the war: the distribution of wool (free of coupons) to those who had husbands or sons in the services (this task was carried out by Mrs Jellett); the distribution of meat pies to agricultural workers who were allowed two per week (Mrs Abbot did this); collecting for the National Savings Stamp Scheme (nobly carried on by Maggie Hall for forty years).

The first school dinners in the country were started in Boxgrove by the Women's Institute. At first if the children took an Oxo cube, the Women's Institute members would make a hot drink for them. Then the Headmaster said he would be prepared to get a school dinner scheme going if he could get the volunteers to cook the meals. Five Women's Institute members volunteered and did the cooking in the infant school. The children paid 3d a day. From this simple, early beginning the idea spread throughout the country.

It is easy to create an idyllic picture of the past - the meadows of Vincent's farm nodding with buttercups, while cows placidly graze; the village pond, which was at the point where the path up to Halnaker crosses The Street; the dirt roads with the occasional horse-drawn vehicle passing by and everything so safe that hens and ducks could wander anywhere, and children could safely roam the countryside for amusement and adventure. Behind this idyll one can sense the hard-working practicality of the people. This was a small, tightly-knit community, coming together for worship and for leisure - such as they had time for. Little changed until mechanisation on the land, and the ravages of the

Second World War changed the spirit and tempo of village life, not suddenly and dramatically but slowly and almost imperceptibly.

Phyllis Norrell and Molly Joyce are two ladies who live today in the almshouses in Boxgrove Village. Phyllis was born in 1923; Molly six months earlier in 1922. Over tea and hot-cross buns they talked about their childhood and the changes that have taken place.

'I lived in an old, thatched cottage up on the corner by the A27,' said Phyllis. 'It's not there now; it was bombed in the war. Then we moved to a cottage in Church Lane. There was a wall in front of the first house, and we used to stand on a stool to look out onto the street. Only farm carts came along it then; sometimes an occasional car. It was just a village lane. There were lots of tramps in the nineteen twenties. Poor people used to come along the A27, sometimes mothers pushing prams, going from the workhouse in Chichester to the other in East Preston. My mother always gave them something to eat. People in those days lived in terror of being given the sack. They nearly all lived in tied cottages and if you lost your job you lost your house. People lived in terror of the workhouse.

'We had no electricity, no running water, no gas. We drew water from the well, and had oil lamps to see by, and a stove to cook on. We went to the village shop for paraffin for the lamps and heaters and accumulators for the wireless. It was a village of small cottages and big houses. The school was there and I went there when I was five. We walked everywhere, of course. Later on I had a bicycle. There was a policeman's house but on the whole we didn't see much of the inmate. On the whole we behaved ourselves. We had to. Discipline was strict, but we were happy.'

Phyllis's father worked at Tangmere, at the airfield. After the war he went to Goodwood and got one of the Goodwood cottages in Church Lane. He enjoyed working for the Duke, the present Duke's grandfather. He was a good employer and Captain Hubbard, the agent, was well respected. Captain Hubbard ran the racecourse and the old Duke would come down to the village and throw sweets to the children in the school. He was always friendly. No-one was frightened of him. Boxgrove was a Goodwood village. The villagers felt part of Goodwood.

The house in Church Lane had no running water until 1954. Electricity was introduced about the same time. At that time a bathroom was added at the back of the house and there was a kitchen tap with a bucket standing under it. There was no kitchen sink. 'Everyone,' said Phyllis, 'was poor. But we were content because we were all the same. There were no flush lavatories, of course, just a bucket which we emptied on to the compost heap and dug into the garden. And the vegetables! We all grew vegetables - no-one dreamed of buying them, and they were all organic: carrots, potatoes, onions, leeks, cabbages. Everything was seasonable. There were no strawberries in January! Everyone shared the produce. "How are you off for beans?" was a familiar question, people helped one another.' Phyllis remembered, '. . . there were no boutiques for children, no fashionable clothes. Everything was made by hand and re-made to fit a younger child. Mrs Woodgate, who lived in one of the old houses in the village street, was the village dressmaker. Everyone went to her. Everything was delivered, of course, in those days as no-one owned a car. People cycled to Chichester for anything special. But shops like the Home and Colonial and the International Stores delivered regularly. Coal was delivered by Mr Blunden. At Halnaker corner was the baker's shop and bread was baked on the premises. The smell was heaven to hungry children.'

Phyllis left school at fifteen, before the war started. She wanted to train as a nanny. But during the war she was a land girl at Aldingbourne sanatorium. She cycled there and back each day. She lived at home with her parents and at seventeen she got diphtheria and went to the fever hospital at Westhampnett. Everyone who caught a serious infectious disease like scarlet fever or diphtheria was sent there. Phyllis recovered, but was weak for a long time afterwards. She worked at Lavant House School and her parents lived on in number seventy Church Lane until they died. People didn't move very often. Society was far more static than it is today. Both her parents died at home; there was no intensive care and people rarely went into hospital. Her father stayed working for the Goodwood estate until he died aged seventy six. People mostly worked locally. Girls went into service, boys worked on the estate. Many people never left the village. The war changed all this, of course. It took people away from the village, extended their horizons. Canadians were billeted in Goodwood House. Tangmere airfield was close at hand, and people watched the Battle of Britain at first hand.

'Always there was the Priory', Phyllis said. 'People went to the Priory. The vicar, the Duke, the schoolmaster and the policeman ran the village.' Phyllis remembers when heating was brought into the Priory through a great boiler which had to be stoked up each day. The organ was hand pumped. Often the boy who did this went to sleep. Phyllis remembers that once, when the organ had to be reconditioned, two wheelbarrows full of toffee papers were taken away.

The almshouses have changed a lot, she remembers. Her grandmother lived in one of them before the war. They were all cottages then, not the flats and cottages of today. There was no warden, no running water, and outside lavatories. (Today they are the garden sheds.) The almshouses were free; no-one paid any rent. They were for the poor of Boxgrove, Tangmere and Easthampnett. They had open fires and people cooked on them in iron pots. The people who lived in these house were often the grandparents of villagers, and they were looked after by their families. The isolation of the elderly, which is a common feature of society today, was very rare. A walk to see granny was a regular activity.

Molly Joyce's childhood was similar to Phyllis's up to the war. She was born on the Goodwood estate at Hat Hill. Her grandparents lived there. During the war her father went into the Navy and Molly's mother lived with the grandparents. Later they moved to Stone Dell. The cottage she lived in has now gone.

Molly walked from Stone Dell to the school. She came down along the Goodwood road, and it took her about an hour to get to school. She brought sandwiches for lunch as there was no canteen. The school was in the centre of the almshouses which is now the modern part where Phyllis lives. The schoolmaster also lived in the middle block. Almshouses and school were together then. Children went to school at five and left at fourteen.

'Schooldays weren't very happy' Molly said. 'Discipline was strict. Children were beaten for stealing apples.' The curriculum was the three R's. They did learn crafts though. The boys learnt to work the loom and dug the gardens. The girls liked weaving. All country children in those days helped in the garden. Boys helped their fathers and girls their mothers. Buckets were emptied on Friday nights out on to the compost heaps. There were no dustbins, but there wasn't much rubbish. The few tins were taken up to the dell and buried. Everything that could be burnt went on the fire or on the compost heap to rot down. Very little was wasted.

'It was hard work for the mothers,' Molly remembered. 'Mothers stayed at home. They were always there when the children came home from school. People weren't fussy about what they ate. They ate everything. Chicken was a luxury and eggs a treat. The day started with a cooked breakfast, usually porridge. The mothers cooked everything, lots of soups, roast on Sundays which lasted for the rest of the week in one form or another, There was no convenience food. There were no washing machines, no washing up machines, no vacuum cleaners. Everything was done by hand. But the families stuck together. Divorce was something people didn't talk about. It was considered shameful because everyone would regard you as a failure. Even when people fell out, which they did, they patched up their quarrels and stuck it out. You married for life. The marriage service was the old service. You promised to love, honour and obey 'till death us do part'.

'Sunday afternoons were the best time of the week. Everyone liked a Sunday afternoon walk and the day usually ended at a pub where the children had a packet of crisps and a bottle of lemonade or ginger beer. There were no canned drinks, of course.'

They had to go to church. Molly remembers being given a book into which she stuck a weekly stamp. Those stamps were very precious. The vicar came to school and took Religious Instruction and prepared children for Confirmation. When asked, 'Did you believe in God?' Molly answered, 'We had to!' Authority was respected. There weren't many rebels.

What, then, was the bad side of life before the war changed everything? There was no money. Phyllis and Molly were both in agreement on this. There was no health scheme. If you were ill you didn't call the doctor - he was too expensive. Most doctors did become family friends and often didn't accept their fee. Illness was frightening. People were often ill for a long time in the days before penicillin. Home remedies were common. Medicine was expensive. Babies were invariably born at home. There was a district nurse who did her rounds on a bicycle. She inspected the school children for nits and impetigo was common. Standards of hygiene were poor. People died of infectious diseases. Tuberculosis, diphtheria, measles and scarlet fever were all serious. There are records that the school was closed for six weeks on several occasions when there was an outbreak of scarlet fever. Septicaemia was a common complication of untreated wounds. Arthritis was common amongst the elderly. Pneumonia was frequently fatal.

Contraception was virtually unknown amongst the village people. Birth control was considered improper for 'nice girls'. There was no sexual freedom. If a girl 'got into trouble' she was blamed. Usually the families took on a collective responsibility for illegitimate children. Families were used to coping with their own disasters.

Molly's and Phyllis's families were members of the Mothers' Union which was well attended in those days. The vicar's wife usually ran it. It goes without saying that you had to be married to belong. There was a Women's Institute and a flourishing Girl Guides and Brownies. The Priory always had a Harvest

Festival and Ascension Day was a holiday. On Empire Day a flag was raised in front of the school and Molly remembers singing the anthem:

Raise the flag on high,
Unfurl it to the breeze.
It's fame spread o'er the earth,
Ruler of the Seas!

People were unashamedly patriotic!

Molly remembers racing at Goodwood as the big event of the year. People dressed up. All the village went and the Trundle was packed with people. Goodwood Week was Boxgrove Week.

When Molly was eighteen she went to Stoke-on-Trent to work in a munitions factory. It was there that she met her husband and a whole new world opened up for her. There is no doubt that the Second World War changed the face of English society. People had a taste of freedom; women, in particular, began to earn money in their own right. No longer were they content to stay at home. When the war ended they weren't willing to revert to their old status.

Figure 51. Pilot Officer W. M. L. Fiske III. Killed in action 17 August 1940.

Molly saw Billy Fiske's funeral. He asked to be buried in Boxgrove churchyard and his grave is frequently visited. He died at the height of the Battle of Britain and his coffin was borne into the churchyard by six members of the groundstaff at Tangmere. Billy's comrades in No 601 Squadron were out fighting the enemy over the Channel when his funeral took place and the survivors didn't return until later that day.

Billy Fiske was an American citizen who joined the Royal Air Force in September 1939 more than two years before America entered the war. He pledged his life and loyalty to the King, George VI and at Tangmere, nearly a year later aged twenty nine, he redeemed that pledge.

In those twenty nine years Fiske, the first American Serviceman in the R.A.F. to lose his life in action, had always lived life to the full. He died a hero's death, surely the way he would have wanted to die, fighting the enemy in the form of a patrol of Junkers 87 about 12,000 feet above the Sussex countryside, at the controls of Hurricane P3358.

Fiske was born on 4 June 1911 in Brooklyn, New York, the son of a wealthy banking family whose ancestors had gone to America from Suffolk in the seventeenth century. He attended school in Chicago and followed his family to France in 1924. He went to Trinity Hall, Cambridge in 1928 where he read Economics and History. Billy packed a lot into the few years between his stay at Trinity Hall and his return to England in 1938 for a spell at the London office of Dillon, Reed & Co. the New York bankers.

He was an accomplished sportsman, well known on the Cresta run at St Moritz and for many years the unbeaten champion. He led the bobsleigh team for the USA in the Winter Olympics of 1928 at St Moritz and the 1932 Winter Olympics at Lake Placid. At this event he carried the flag for the Americans at the opening ceremonies, presided over by Governor Franklin D. Roosevelt of New York. He was invited, but declined, to lead the bobsleigh team in the 1936 Winter Olympics. The Billy Fiske trophy is named for him, the youngest Gold Medal winner, at the age of sixteen, in the sport.

He was also a keen golfer, and at Cambridge and Mildenhall he became a well known figure driving to the golf course at high speed on the long straight roads, in his 4$^{1}/_{2}$ litre open Bentley, in British racing green, complete with bonnet strap and projecting supercharger. He also managed to fit in a bit of film making in Tahiti.

He learnt to fly at an aerodrome near London and married Rose, the former Countess of Warwick, at Maidenhead in 1938. She remembers 'the big day when he was allowed to take me in an open two seater' (aircraft) on a flight to Le Touquet which ended at Deauville because of an oil leak that splattered over the windscreen and so hindered navigation.

Early in 1939 Billy was recalled to his firm's New York office shortly before England declared war on Germany on 3 September. An English friend working in New York, Mr W.P.Clyde, an RAF reservist and a member of 601 (County of London) Auxiliary Air Force Squadron, talked him into sailing back to England with him on the Aquitania on 30 August. In his diary, Billy Fiske records that 'I believe I can lay claim to being the first US citizen to join the RAF in England after the outbreak of hostilities.' He did not realise he was writing his epitaph. He also knew when he sailed from America that, as the regulations stood at the time, 'no person, not a British citizen and a son of British citizens, could be eligible for any position whatsoever in the Air Force'. So he worked out a plan to pass himself off as a Canadian of Canadian parentage. But, even so, he found that joining the RAF was harder than he anticipated and it was luck and knowing the right people which eventually got him an interview with a high-ranking RAF officer. We know he was nervous before the interview as he records in his diary that he played a round of golf at Roehampton to give himself a 'healthy look'. He notes, 'Needless to say, for once I had a quiet Saturday night - I didn't want to have eyes looking like blood-stained oysters the next day.'

He passed his interview and full of the joy of life went on to No 10 Elementary Flying Training School, Yatesbury, Wiltshire. After Yatesbury, Billy moved to the Flying Training school at Brize Norton, Oxfordshire and with his wife took a small house at nearby Minster Lovell. At Brize Norton on 12 April 1940 he became Acting Pilot Officer Fiske and on 12 July was posted to No 601 (County of London) Auxiliary Air Force Squadron at Tangmere. This squadron was variously known as the Legionnaires and the Millionaires Squadron, for it had been at White's Club, St James, in 1924 that Lord Edward Grosvenor selected members of the Club to serve under him in 601. Billy now had one month to live. At Tangmere there was some apprehension in 601 about taking 'this untried American adventurer...' but Billy made no pretensions about his flying skill and was soon accepted. With typical gusto he threw himself into training and on 20th July he undertook two operational 'take-offs' in quick succession in Hurricane L1951 late in the afternoon. An American radio commentator said in 1942 that Billy Fiske, during his fleeting service with 601, destroyed six enemy aircraft, the first being a Heinkel. Billy enjoyed flying Hurricanes. No doubt the aircraft, with 100 gallons of petrol tucked away in tanks close to the pilot seat and an engine capable of taking it up to 335 mph, reminded him of his Bentley.

Then came the last flight. On 16 August, Tangmere aerodrome was singled out for attack by German dive-bombers. The Operations Record book of No 601 Squadron records that he took off in Hurricane P3358 at 12.25 pm. Squadron Leader Sir Archibald Hope Bt led the Squadron and they were ordered to patrol over Tangmere at about 12,000ft.

The dive-bombers, Junkers 87, were seen to cross the coast east of Selsey Bill. Then the Stukas, as they were called, started to dive on Tangmere and after several sharp individual combats, known as dogfights, the enemy were eventually chased out over the coast around Pagham Harbour.

When the Hurricanes started to land back at Tangmere, Billy Fiske's was seen 'to glide over the boundary and land on it's belly'. The Operations Record Book stated 'Pilot Officer Fiske was seen to land on the aerodrome and his aircraft immediately caught fire. He was taken from the machine but sustained severe burns . . .' He was taken to the Royal West Sussex Hospital in Chichester but died forty eight hours later from shock.

The funeral took place on 20 August 1940. As the coffin, covered with the Union Jack and the Stars and Stripes, was borne on a bier to Boxgrove Priory Church the Central Band of the RAF played funeral marches. Overhead the Battle of Britain raged on. The coffin was borne into the churchyard by six members of the ground staff at Tangmere. Billy's comrades, although they did not land back at Tangmere until late that day, came with him on his last journey to Boxgrove.

In the south-east corner of Boxgrove graveyard there is a fine headstone to the memory of Pilot Officer Bill Fiske. On either side of his grave lie two soldiers, a Sapper in the Royal Engineers and a Corporal in the east Lancashire Regiment. Fiske's grave is distinguished by a small Stars and Stripes flag. This was the man who Lt Col J T C Moore-Brabazon (later Lord Brabazon of Tara) honoured with the words in a newspaper tribute, 'We thank America for sending us the perfect sportsman. Many of us would have given our lives for Billy.'

On 4 July (Independence Day) 1941 a tablet in his honour was unveiled in the crypt of St Pauls Cathedral. At the unveiling Sir Archibald Sinclair, Secretary of State for Air, said 'Here was a young man for whom life held much. Under no kind of compulsion he came to fight for Britain. He came and he fought and he died.'

Billy Fiske, sportsman, golden boy, fighter pilot, is rightly honoured as the first American Airman in British Service to die in the Second World War. Many Americans followed him. By 1941 there were enough American pilots in the RAF to form the three squadrons Nos 71, 121 and 132.

Today Boxgrove is a busy, pretty village. There is one main street which links the A27 with the A285, the Roman Stane Street, and during the day the noise of traffic is virtually continuous as cars cut through the village on their way to Halnaker, Petworth, Guildford and London (see XXV in colour section). On either side of the street there are houses, some old cottages, once the homes of people who worked on the Goodwood estate, some new houses set back from the road behind an attractive green, fringed with silver birch trees, and other very new houses built only last year. At the Halnaker end of the village there are the Countess of Derby's almshouses built in 1742, and a school dating from the same time. Since the war there has been extensive building of houses down

Crouch Cross Lane. There is a shop and post office which is well used both by villagers and people passing through. Always there are lots of cars parked outside the shop and sometimes the half-hourly buses going to Chichester and Brighton have a job squeezing past them (see XXIV in colour section). The road leading up to the Priory has some attractive old cottages, and set back in the fields behind the Priory is a small business development and a couple of elegant private houses. But the advent of popular motoring together with the war has changed the static nature of village life.

Today the people who have moved into the new houses go off to work in the morning in their cars, sometimes leaving as early as six o'clock and heading for the southern cities or even London. Children are driven to school. They are no longer free as they were before the war when everyone in the community was known and children felt safe (see XXVI in colour section).

There is still, though, a sense of community. People still walk their dogs along the same paths which Molly and Phyllis walked along as children. The shop is now the centre of village life and on fine days groups of people stand talking together along The Street just as they always did. Now we are richer, our children are better dressed, our teenagers wear fashionable clothes and everyone drives to work and to find entertainment. Our houses are centrally heated and full of labour saving gadgets. Motor cars stand parked outside the houses or tucked away in garages. People go by car or bus into Chichester to one of the many supermarkets which weren't there before the war. Families are scattered; many people live on their own and don't expect their children to come very often once they have grown up and left home. The Priory is still there for baptisms, marriages and funerals. No longer do people feel obliged to go there every Sunday. Many people, however, do come from all over West Sussex to attend the services as the motor car brings them the freedom to choose which church they want to attend; something unheard of in pre-war days.

'Are we happier?' Mollie and Phyllis sound doubtful. We have all these material possessions and there is no doubt that people live longer and are better looked after by Social Services. But something has gone they both agreed. Society is harder and loneliness is a major problem. Life cannot stand still, but we can keep alive the memory of life as it was. The great events of history, and the great men and women, they have been and will continue to be written about. But the lives of ordinary people are not so closely recorded. What has been written here is just a small part of the collective memory of those who lived through this period, between 1885 and 1945.